First World War
and Army of Occupation
War Diary
France, Belgium and Germany

3 CAVALRY DIVISION
Headquarters, Branches and Services
Royal Army Veterinary Corps
Assistant Director Veterinary Services
23 November 1915 - 30 April 1919

WO95/1145/3

The Naval & Military Press Ltd
www.nmarchive.com
Published in association with The National Archives

Published by

The Naval & Military Press Ltd

Unit 10 Ridgewood Industrial Park,

Uckfield, East Sussex,

TN22 5QE England

Tel: +44 (0) 1825 749494

www.naval-military-press.com

www.nmarchive.com

This diary has been reprinted in facsimile from the original. Any imperfections are inevitably reproduced and the quality may fall short of modern type and cartographic standards.

© **Crown Copyright**
Images reproduced by permission of The National Archives, London, England, 2015.

Contents

Document type	Place/Title	Date From	Date To
Heading	WO95/1145/3		
Heading	1915-1919 3rd Cavalry Division. Asst Dir. Vety Services Nov 1915-Apl 1919		
Heading	War Diary of A.D.V.S. 3rd Cavalry Division Nov to December-1915 to Apl 1919		
War Diary	Fruges	23/11/1915	31/12/1915
Heading	War Diary of A.D.V.S. 3rd Cavalry. Divn From 1st Jan 1915 To 29 February 1916 Vol IA & II		
War Diary	Fruges	01/01/1916	29/02/1916
War Diary	La Neuville	01/07/1916	01/07/1916
War Diary	Halancourt	04/07/1916	04/07/1916
War Diary	Daours	08/07/1916	18/07/1916
War Diary	Quesnoy	01/08/1916	01/08/1916
War Diary	Yvrench	02/08/1916	02/08/1916
War Diary	Ligescourt	04/08/1916	04/08/1916
War Diary	Fruges	05/08/1916	31/08/1916
War Diary	Brevillers	30/09/1916	30/09/1916
War Diary	La Houssoie	31/10/1916	30/11/1916
War Diary	Trepied	31/12/1916	31/03/1917
War Diary	Ligescourt	30/04/1917	30/04/1917
Miscellaneous	D D V S Cav Corps	16/04/1917	16/04/1917
War Diary	Flamicourt	31/05/1917	30/06/1917
War Diary	Busnes	31/08/1917	30/09/1917
War Diary	Domart En Ponthieu	31/10/1917	31/10/1917
War Diary	Corbie	09/12/1917	09/12/1917
War Diary	Domart-En-Ponthieu	31/12/1917	31/12/1917
War Diary	Monchy Lagache	31/01/1918	28/02/1918
War Diary	Rivery Amiens	07/04/1918	07/04/1918
War Diary	Pernes	30/04/1918	30/04/1918
Miscellaneous	Extract from Weekly Technical Report for W/E 4-4-18		
War Diary	Yzeux	31/05/1918	06/08/1918
War Diary	Pont Le Metz	07/08/1918	19/08/1918
War Diary	Yzeux	20/08/1918	25/08/1918
War Diary	Fountain L'Etalon	26/08/1918	26/08/1918
War Diary	Wail	27/08/1918	31/08/1918
War Diary	Wailly	01/09/1918	21/09/1918
War Diary	Fountain L'Etalon	22/09/1918	25/09/1918
War Diary	Marrine	26/09/1918	27/09/1918
War Diary	Clary	28/09/1918	29/09/1918
War Diary	Povilly	30/09/1918	13/10/1918
War Diary	Bois de Hennois	14/10/1918	18/11/1918
War Diary	Enghien	19/11/1918	22/11/1918
War Diary	Perwez	23/11/1918	24/11/1918
War Diary	Maleves-Ste.	25/11/1918	25/11/1918
War Diary	Marie-Wastines	26/11/1918	30/11/1918
War Diary	Field	01/12/1918	16/12/1918
War Diary	Soaeit Tinlot	17/12/1918	31/12/1918
War Diary	Nandrin	01/01/1919	31/03/1919
War Diary	Amay	01/04/1919	23/04/1919
War Diary	Engis	24/04/1919	30/04/1919

WO 95/1145(3)

1915-1919
3RD CAVALRY DIVISION

ASST DIR. VETY SERVICES

NOV 1915 - APL 1919

WAR DIARY

OF

A.D.V.S.

3rd CAVALRY DIVISION

Nov &
December - 1915.
to
April 1919

Army Form C. 2118.

A.D.V.S. WAR DIARY Vol I
3rd Cav Div
INTELLIGENCE SUMMARY.
23-11-15 — 31-12-15

Place	Date	Hour	Summary of Events and Information	Remarks and references to Appendices
FRUGES	23-11-15	4.05pm	Arrived from DEVRES in 9° Cav. Bvy Car guiding 9 Car. Bvy: reported to AA+QMG 3°Cav Div Eng.	
"	24-11-15		Took over duties A.D.V.S. 3° Cav. Div from Capt Richardson A.V.C. (T.F.) acting A.D.V.S. Visited A.D.V.S. Gbr. Corps office at LUMBRES, 14" M.V.S. at VERDURE, HERLY 20" M.V.S. at RIMBOVAL, 13" M.V.S. at PETIT BEAURANVILLE in a 3° Cav. Div motor car.	
"	25-11-15		A.D.V.S. Car. Corps came to office described duties A D V S 3° Car. Div. Eng.	
"	26-11-15		Visits 14. M.V.S. suspicious Skin case, inspected suspicious Skin cases & Jumbers inspect in 10" Hussars at MATRINGHAM & COYECQUE in Car lent by AA+QMG. Annual pooled car not available. Eng.	
"	27-11-15		Visits 14.M.V.S. at VERDURE HERLY on horseback, unable to obtain a divisional pooled car therefore could not visit & inspect Leicestershire Geomanry. Studied office front correspondence. Eng.	
"	28-11-15		Visited CREQUY interviewed Lt. Johnston A.V.C. L 6° Car. Bvy; then to RIMBOVAL cars Capt. J.B. Walker L 7° Bvyade and inspected sick horses in 20"M.V.S. visited OFFIN to inspect 2 chargers then to PETIT BEAURANVILLE and inspected 13"M.V.S. Eng.	

Army Form C. 2118.

WAR DIARY
or
INTELLIGENCE SUMMARY.
(Erase heading not required.)

Instructions regarding War Diaries and Intelligence Summaries are contained in F.S. Regs., Part II. and the Staff Manual respectively. Title pages will be prepared in manuscript.

Place	Date	Hour	Summary of Events and Information	Remarks and references to Appendices
FRUGES	29/11/15		Visited 14" V.M.S. at VERDURE HERLY inspecting mange suspected horses prepared for evacuation. Car again unobtainable, necessary duties of inspection again postponed. enc.	
"	30/11/15		Visited with A.D.V.S. Cav. Corps 2 Horses 3" D. G's at OFFIN, 20 M.V.S. and 14" M.V.S. inspecting sick horses. enc.	
"	1/12/15		Visited CREQUY inspected Horse & Sent it to No 13 M.V.S. mange suspect from "Royals"	
"	2/12/15		Visited 3" Field Squadron R E horse inspection enc.	
"	3/12/15		Visited 10" Hussars at S! MICHEL inspected horses with skin diseases enc.	
"			With A.D.S. Cav. Corps visited HEQUELIERS inspecting horses of 7" Cav. Brig. Head Quarters 7" Cav. Field Amb. 2" Life Guards; then to WICQUINGHEM inspecting Leicestershire Yeomanry enc.	
"	4/12/15		With A.D.S. Cav. Corps visited RUMILLY inspecting 1st Life Guards, then to ESSONVAL inspecting 'K' Batt. R.H.A.	enc.
"	5/12/15		Visited unaffected horses in Nos 13,14 & 20 Vet. Mobile Sections	enc.
"	6/12/15		With A.D.V.S. Cav. Corps visited OFFIN inspected 3" D. G's and then to HESMOND and inspected North Somerset Yeomanry	enc.
"	7/12/15		Visited RUMILLY near HEQUELIERS inspecting horses H/propinquity of Angel horse affected with pneumonia; isolated item from B Sqdrn 1st Life Guards.	enc.

WAR DIARY
or
INTELLIGENCE SUMMARY.

Army Form C. 2118.

Place	Date	Hour	Summary of Events and Information	Remarks and references to Appendices
FRUGES	8/12/15		Visited ROYON inspecting horses of 6° Cav. Bde. H.2., TORCY inspecting "C" Batt. R.H.A. here was joined by A.D.V.S, Cav. Corps & D.A.D.R. Cav. Corps then to CREQUY inspecting 1st Royal Dragoons; and. In the afternoon visited EMBRY inspecting horses of ESSEX YEO. with Shoin irritation and to RIMBOVAL (20° M.V.S.) inspecting horses for evacuation E.U.6.	
"	9/12/15		Inspected in FRUGES following horses belonging to 3rd Cav. Div. 81st C.A.S.C. A.P.M's, 3rd Cav. Div. H.2., 3° Sig. Squadron, A.H.T.Co. A.S.C., 6° Cav. Field Amb., also 6° Cav. Batt. R.E. Stationed in FRUGES. Visited 14° M.V.S. at VERDURE HURLY inspecting horses prior to evacuation EU.6.	
"	10/12/15		Inspected in FRUGES horses of 4° Bde. R.H.A. H.2s. at COUPELLE-VIELLE 3° Field Squadron R.E. at COUPELLE-NEUVE 4° Bde. Amm. Column Visited at PETIT BEAURANVILLE 13° M.V.S. inspected horses prior to evacuation. Inspected at OFFIN 3 horses of 3° D.G's with irritable chrens. EU.6.	
"	11/12/15		Visited RIMBOVAL inspecting horses prior to evacuation at 20° M.V.S. and 2 horses Shoin, then to EMBRY inspecting horses shoin of ESSEX YEO. EU.6.	

Army Form C. 2118.

WAR DIARY
or
INTELLIGENCE SUMMARY.
(Erase heading not required.)

Instructions regarding War Diaries and Intelligence Summaries are contained in F. S. Regs., Part II. and the Staff Manual respectively. Title pages will be prepared in manuscript.

Place	Date	Hour	Summary of Events and Information	Remarks and references to Appendices
FRUGES	12/12/15		Visited Vety. Lieut. Smith R.H.G. at HUMBERT and held a consultation re horses of 10th Royal Hussars & Royal Horse Guards, then motored to LUMBRES to attend a conference of A.D.V.S. Cavalry Corps to discuss application of intra-palpebral mallein test to all horses of Cavalry Corps; decided to apply test to Brigades concurrently, units successively, as early as syringes + mallein were available, with concurrence of G.O.C. Cav. Divs. & C.B.	
	13/12/15		Visited No 13 Vety. Hospital at Neufchatel with Lieut. Ellison Davis + Capt. Walker to study the method of inoculating large numbers of horses at one time with the intra-palpebral method of malleinisation; every assistance was given by Major (actg.) Simms + his staff specially Lieut. Wright + a most instructive afternoon was spent.	cert.
	14/12/15		Visited Nos. 13 + 14 M.V.S. inoculated horses to be evacuated.	cert.
	15/12/15		Submitted to A.A. & LMG 3rd War Ser. programme with dates time & places for testing the 6th + 7th Cav. Bdes. Again visited No 13 Vet. Hospital at Neufchatel with Capt. Richardson, Lieut. R.C. Johnston + Vety. Lieut. Smith R.H.G. for instruction in palpebral mallein test. sup	cert.

WAR DIARY
of
INTELLIGENCE SUMMARY.
(Erase heading not required.)

Army Form C. 2118.

Place	Date	Hour	Summary of Events and Information	Remarks and references to Appendices
FRUGES	16/12/15		Visited ROMILLY taking Capt. Walker 700 doses Mallein for 2nd Life Guards 7th Cav Bde. Visited RIMBOVAL taking Lieut Davis 700 doses Mallein for 6" Cav. Bde.; completed inoculation programme for 8th Cav. Bde.; left 700 doses Mallein for 1st Royal Dragoons 6th Cav. Bde. with Lieut Gore Johnston at C.R.O.C.R.S.	
"	17/12/15		Great difficulty in obtaining use of a car owing to break downs, and short supply of units. Following were inoculated with infra-glyphoid method of Mallein injection 3rd Cav. Div. Headquarters, 81 Coy. A.S.C. 3rd Signal Squadron R.E. Auxilliary H.T. Coy. 6 Cav field Amb. & 4" Bde R.H.A. Headquarters, 1st Royal Dragoons, 2nd Life Guards.	exc.
"	18/12/15		Inspection of inoculated units at 24 hrs after the injection, reinoculation of North Somerset Yeo., "G" Batt. R.H.A.	exc.
"	19/12/15		Inspection of inoculated units at 24 & 48 hours. Inor. of 3rd D. G's + Essex Yeo.	exc.
"	20/12/15		Inspections as before + inoc. of Div. Am. Col., "C" Batt. R.H.A. 6 Cav Bde Headquarters, 1st Life Guards, and Royal Horse Guards; outbreak of F+M Disease at MARANT in billets	exc.
"	21/12/15		Inspections as before + inoc. of 3rd Field Squadron R.E. officially MSR.48.; Farm closed up + left mined.	exc.
"	22/12/15		Inspections as before + inoc., no 13 V.M.S.	exc.
"	23/12/15		Inspections as before + inoc. 7 C.B.F.A., 7 C. Bde H.A. Quarters, "K" Bn R.H.A., 14 V.M.S.	exc.

WAR DIARY
or
INTELLIGENCE SUMMARY.
(Erase heading not required.)

Army Form C. 2118.

Place	Date	Hour	Summary of Events and Information	Remarks and references to Appendices
FRUGES	24/12/15		Inspections of C.F. Amb, J.C. Fide Hos Sections, "K"Batt R.H.A., 14" V.M.S. Coy	
	25/12/15		" " J.C.F. " " " " K " " " " Coy	
	26/12/15		Inspected 2 Horse "K" Batt at Gournay	
	27/12/15		Inspected 1 Horse K Batt R.H.A. at GOURNAY, went at 6 PM V.M.S. under canvas	
	28/12/15		Inspected at HUMBERT horses of 10" howrs, No 20 V.M.S. at RIMBOVAL Coy.	
	29/12/15		Inve Leinster Yeo. with Malein, visited HUMBERT with ADVS Cav Corps inspecting Shire cases also at 20YMS at RIMBOVAL sub.	
	30/12/15		Visited & inspected Leinster Yeo at HERLY, VERDURE and WICQUINHEM sub.	
	31/12/15		Visited & inspected Leinster Yeo also visited 3" D.G.s at OFFIN and No 13 M.V.S. at PETIT BEAERANVILLE inspecting many inspects. sub.	

CONFIDENTIAL

WAR DIARY

OF

A.D.V.S. 3RD CAVALRY DIV.N

FROM 1st November 1915
TO 29th February 1916

Vol. I & II

WAR DIARY
or
INTELLIGENCE SUMMARY.
(Erase heading not required.)

Army Form C. 2118.

Place	Date	Hour	Summary of Events and Information	Remarks and references to Appendices
FRUGES	1/7/16		Visited & inspected glanders suspects in Leicester Yeo. at VERDURE & WICQUINGHEM and inspected 2 mange suspects at No 14 M.V.S.	
	2/7/16		Visited at RIMBOVAL the 20ᵗʰ M.V.S. inspecting horse prisoners & evacuation Estab.	
	3/7/16		Visited 3ʳᵈ Hill Squadron inspecting mange suspects at GOUPELLE NEUVE, hospital with mallein belonging to 2ⁿᵈ Life Guards at HUCAVELIERS & horses for evacuation at 14 M.V.S at VERDURE Estab.	
	4/7/16		Inspected horses for evacuation at No 13 M.V.S. at PETIT BEAUVAINVILLE esb.	
			" horses as mange suspects 3ʳᵈ D.G.s at OFFIN esb.	
	5/7/16		Visited 10ᵗʰ Royal Hussars at HUMBERT inspecting mange suspects. Esb.	
	6/7/16		Inspected in FRUGES Divisional Troops: visited 14 M.V.S. for microscopic investigation of suspicious skin cases Estab.	
	7/7/16		Visited 1ˢᵗ & 2ⁿᵈ Life Guards inspecting sick horses at RUMILLY & HECRULIERS. inspected horses & Shire in Leics. Yeo., at HERLY esb.	
	8/7/16		Inspected at No 13 M.V.S. under mach'. Mallein test 2 horses 1ʳᵈ D's Hussars of 3ʳᵈ D.G's & 1 horse of N. Somerset Yeo. all were non-reactors then visited 14 M.V.S. at VERDURE 5 horses from Leics by co preparatory of mange. Esb.	

Army Form C. 2118.

WAR DIARY
or
INTELLIGENCE SUMMARY.
(Erase heading not required.)

Instructions regarding War Diaries and Intelligence Summaries are contained in F. S. Regs., Part II. and the Staff Manual respectively. Title pages will be prepared in manuscript.

Place	Date	Hour	Summary of Events and Information	Remarks and references to Appendices
Fruges	9/1/16		Visited 20 M.V.S. at RIMBOVAL inspecting horses previous to evacuation	
	10/1/16		Inspected at 14 M.V.S. Suspicious cases of mange with A.D.V.S. Cav. Corps.	
	11/1/16		Inspected mange suspects at 1st Royal Dragoons, 3rd D. Gds, & 13 M.V.S. also horses for remounts	
	12/1/16		Inspected mange suspects at EMBRY and RIMBOVAL — Essex Yeo.	
	13/1/16		Inspected horses of 10th Royal Hussars at HUMBERT & 20 M.V.S.	
	14/1/16		Inspected horses of 1st R. D's at CREQUY, 6 Cav. Bde Hors Quarters at ROYON & 20 M.V.S. RIMBOVAL	
	15/1/16		Inoculated 13 horses of Leicester Yeo. with Mallein Reck test (after the French "eye" test)	
	16/1/16		Inspected horses at 20 M.V.S.	
	17/1/16		Inspected 13 horses of Leicester Yeo. under Mallein test.	
			Inspected horses 3rd Field Squadron R.E.	
	18/1/16		Visited Leicester Yeo. at HERLY. 7 horses passed Mallein test. 3 reacted & post-mortem needed of positive lesions, 3 doubtful reactors were isolated for retesting.	
	19/1/16		Visited 10th R. Hussars at HUMBERT inspecting mange suspects	
	20/1/16		Prepared full report for A.D.V.S. Cav. Corps on infra palpebral mallein test of 3rd Cav. Div re	
	21/1/16		Attended Horse Cavalry Parade at HUCQUELIERS held by D.A.D.R. Cav. Corps for horses of 1st & 2nd Life Guards & Leicester Yeo.	

Army Form C. 2118.

WAR DIARY
or
INTELLIGENCE SUMMARY.
(Erase heading not required.)

Instructions regarding War Diaries and Intelligence Summaries are contained in F. S. Regs., Part II. and the Staff Manual respectively. Title pages will be prepared in manuscript.

Place	Date	Hour	Summary of Events and Information	Remarks and references to Appendices
FRUGES	22/1/16		Inspected horses at 20 M.V.S. Cav6.	
	23/1/16		Entries taken over by Capt. Davis D.C. 20 M.V.S. during temporary absence. Cav6.	
	1/2/16		Resumed duty. Cav6.	
	2/2/16		Visited by A.D.V.S. Cav. Corps: inspected horses at 14 M.V.S. Cav6.	
	3/2/16		Inspected skin cases of 1st R.D. at CREQUY, N. Somerset Yeo. at LEBIEZ, 3rd R.D's at OFFIN & at 13th M.V.S. Cav6.	
	4/2/16		Inspected skin cases at HOMBERT of 10th R. Hussars, at POTTIER of Essex Yeo. & at 20 M.V.S. RIMBOVAL of 10th R. Hussars; on this day my duties were considerably impeded by being unable to obtain use of a motor car. Cav6	
	5/2/16		Inspected horses of 3rd Field Squadron R.E. at CAPELLE NOUVELLE Cav6.	
	6/2/16		Inspected horses for evacuation at 20 M.V.S. Cav6.	
	7/2/16		Inspected with A.D.V.S. Cav6.	
	8/2/16		Inspected with A.D.V.S. Cavalry Corps Euphistis mange cases at 20 M.V.S. & at HOMBERT belonging to 10th Royal Hussars. Cav6. & also at 14 M.V.S. at BELLEVUE & Major Edwards A.V.C. accompanied A.D.V.S. Cav. Corps preparatory to taking over his appointment. Cav6.	
	9/2/16		Inspected suspicious skin cases in Cav. Bde. belonging to 3rd Dragoon Guards & N. Somerset Yeo. Cav6.	

Army Form C. 2118.

WAR DIARY
or
INTELLIGENCE SUMMARY.
(Erase heading not required.)

Instructions regarding War Diaries and Intelligence Summaries are contained in F. S. Regs., Part II. and the Staff Manual respectively. Title pages will be prepared in manuscript.

Place	Date	Hour	Summary of Events and Information	Remarks and references to Appendices
FRUGES	10/2/16		Visited 1st Life Guards at RUMILLY inspecting sick horses also C Squadron Sn.6.	
	11/2/16		Inspected 3 Field Squadron R.E. suspicious skin cases. Cn6	
	12/2/16		Inspected at 14 M.V.S. horses of Leinster Yeo. with suspicious Skin Cnb.	
	13/2/16		Inspected 3rd Field Squadron R.E. 3 horses with Styxmia, 3 with Anyonema Cnb. Visited 2 OMVS at RIMBOVAL inspecting horses for evacuation & then 6th ECavaliers inspecting sick horses of 2nd Life Guards. Sn.6.	
	14/2/16		Inspected horses for evacuation at 14 M.V.S. & sick horses at 3rd Field Squadron R.E. Sn6.	
	15/2/16		Visited with Lt.-Col. W.E. Edwards DDVS Cav. Corps 14.M.V.S. evacuating 3 mange suspects from Leinster Yeo.; then we visited 10th R. Hussars at HUMBERT sending 3 mange suspects to 20 M.V.S. for observation; then we visited 20 M.V.S. evacuating 4 horses of 10th Royal Hussars as mange suspects.	
	16/2/16		Visited 3rd D. H/q at OFFIN & 13 M.V.S. inspecting horses for evacuation Sn.6.	
	17/2/16		Inspected Leinster Yeo. horses at VERDURE isolating 3 mange suspects R.E. Sn6	
	18/2/16		Visited sick horses at 3rd Field Squadron R.E. Sn6. Day spent in routine office work.	
	19/2/16		Visited 3rd D.G./s at OFFIN & 13 M.V.S. inspecting mange suspects Sn.6.	

Army Form C. 2118.

WAR DIARY
or
INTELLIGENCE SUMMARY.
(Erase heading not required.)

Instructions regarding War Diaries and Intelligence Summaries are contained in F. S. Regs., Part II. and the Staff Manual respectively. Title pages will be prepared in manuscript.

Place	Date	Hour	Summary of Events and Information	Remarks and references to Appendices
FRUGES	20/2/16		Visited 20 M.V.S. at RIMBOVAL inspecting horses for evacuation & N.Somerset Yeomanry at HESMOND inspecting 2 mange suspects. Sub.	
	21/2/16		Visited 14 M.V.S. inspecting horses for evacuation at BELLEVUE, the Leicestershire Yeo. at VERDURE including 2 mange suspects and 3rd Field Squadron R.E. at COUPELLE NEUVE Sub	
	22/2/16		Visited 1st Royal Dragoons at CREQUY inspecting 3 mange suspects, N. Somerset Yeo. at HESMOND inspecting 4 mange suspects, and 13 M.V.S. at PETIT BEAUVANVILLE inspecting horses for evacuation. Sub.	
	23/2/16		Roads snowed up, unable to travel; Sub.	
	24/2/16		With D.D.V.S. Cavalry Corps visited 14 M.V.S. at BELLEVUE + Leicesters Yeo at VERDURE inspecting mange suspects; also at 10th R. HUSSARS at HUMBERT + 20 M.V.S. at RIMBOVAL. Sub.	
	25/2/16		Heavy snow storms: travelling impossible Sub.	
	26/2/16		Visited CREQUY inspecting 3 horses of Argyles + LE BIEZ inspecting 4 horses of N Somerset Yeo. Sub.	
	27/2/16		Visited 20" M.V.S. inspecting horses for evacuation Sub.	
	28/2/16		Visited 14 M.V.S at BELLVUE inspecting horses for evacuation + Leicester Yeo at VERDURE Sub.	
	29/2/16		Visited Argyles at Crequy, N. Somerset Yeo at LE BIEZ, 3 D Yo at OFFIN + Royal Horse Guards at MARENLA. Sub.	

A.D.V.S.
3 Cav Div

WAR DIARY
or
INTELLIGENCE SUMMARY
(Erase heading not required.)

Army Form C. 2118.
Vol 7

Hour, Date, Place	Summary of Events and Information	Remarks and references to Appendices
LA NEUVILLE. 1-7-16.	Take over duties of A.D.V.S. 3rd Cav. Div.n from Major W. B. Edwards A.V.C.	W. B. Edwards A.V.C.
HAHNCOURT. 4-7-16.	Division moved to W. Headquarters Halancourt.	
DAOURS 8-7-16	Divisional Hd Qrs. from Halancourt to Daours	
DAOURS 14 July to 18. July	Divisits' glassing to' between these dates	
QUESNOY. 1. Aug. 1916.	Division moving Wart - Layer Daours two H.Q. morning. Nothing of importance or necessary to record in connection with the Vet.ry. administration of the Division has occurred during the month of July 1916	

C.H.Hylton 98Huffs. Maj. A.V.C.
A.D.V.S.
3rd Cav. Div.

WAR DIARY or INTELLIGENCE SUMMARY

Army Form C. 2118.

ADMS

Hour, Date, Place	Summary of Events and Information	Remarks and references to Appendices
QUESNOY. 1.Aug.1916	Divisional Hd.Qrs. moved today from DROUDS to QUESNOY.	
YVRENCH. 2. Aug.'16	Division moved to STRIQUIER area. Hd.Qrs. to YVRENCH.	
LIGESCOURT. 4. "	Divisional Hd.Qrs. from YVRENCH to Ligescourt, en route to the FRUGES area.	
FRUGES. 5. " "	" " " at TRAMECOURT & FRUGES.	
" 31. " "	The Division has remained in this area since the 5th inst. Have inspected the majority of the horses of the Division during tomorrow. Taken on the whole they are in fair condition, but very few of them carrying any surplus flesh. The condition of the horses of the 3rd Field of Arty R.E. is about the poorest of any in the Division. Their strength is about 2,15. On Aug. 22nd received information that of Remounts recently received (Aug. 12th) from No.1 V.S. Remount Depot, Rouen had come from a Remount Brigade in which a dangerous case of clinical Glanders had since been discovered. These were tested with Mallein with a negative result. Col Hartley D.D.V.S. 3rd Army inspected horses for Casting for "Remount" rejoined on the 6th & the 7 Brigades on Aug. 7. 4 of the 7 H.Q.B. & Divisional Troops on Aug. 21 &.— The general health of the horses has been satisfactory. 23. Have been executed during tomonth for veterinary reasons — of these 107 were for debility and 26 for Skin disease. The new Divine 98 bring for renous reasons — Lameness, Kicks of similar accidents. The majority being of a surgical nature. Capt Richardson V.C. H.O. to V.C. Divine Hops OHHHHler goliffg Transferred to No.3225 ds on the 27th inst. Maj. A.V.C. And Cap. Phibbs A.V.C. arrived and C.D.V.S. 3rd Army Division Reported on the 30th inst.	

1247 W 3299 200,000 (E) 8/14 J.R.C. & A. Forms/C. 2118.11.

A.D.V.S. 3 Cav Div
Army Form C. 2118.

WAR DIARY
or
INTELLIGENCE SUMMARY
(Erase heading not required.) Sept. 1916.

Hour, Date, Place	Summary of Events and Information	Remarks and references to Appendices
BREVILLER'S 30. Sept 1916.	The Division has been moving between different areas during the month & on the 10th it came under the administration of the Cavalry Corps. The health & condition of the horses has been satisfactory — 236 have been evacuated during the month, of which 46 have been for Debility & 5 for Mange or suspected mange — 1 for Ringworm. Attended a Conference at the offices of D.D.V.S. Fourth Army on the 11th inst, at which it was decided that in the event of Cavalry coming into action, Mobile Veterinary Sections should be detached from their Brigades & become Divisional troops & before under the orders of a D.V.S.	A.D.V.S. 3rd Cavalry Div Capt W Wolffe Major RAVC A.D.V.S. 3rd Cavalry Div

WAR DIARY
or
INTELLIGENCE SUMMARY

Army Form C. 2118.

A.D.V.S. 12

October 1916.

Vol.

Hour, Date, Place	Summary of Events and Information	Remarks and references to Appendices
LA HOUSSOIE. 31 Oct 1916.	The health & condition of the horses of the Division continues satisfactory. 131 have been evacuated during the month for Vety. reasons. Of these 27 have been for debility, and 5 for Mange. Apart from these there have been no cases of contagious or infectious disease, except that Ringworm is somewhat at present in the 3rd Bde. R.H.A. On Oct 31st all artillery H.Q. & the R.H.A. Ammn. Col. to C.O. & R Batteries R.H.A. became detached from the Divn & our new attachés to 63rd R.N. Divn. Capt. W.E. Phelps A.V.C. accompanies these Units in Veterinary charge.	Capt. H. Tolliffe. Maj. A.V.C. A.D.V.S. 3rd Cav. Divn.

Army Form C. 2118.

A.D.V.S.

WAR DIARY
INTELLIGENCE SUMMARY
(Erase heading not required.)

Hour, Date, Place	Summary of Events and Information	Remarks and references to Appendices
LA HOUSSOIE. 30. Nov 1916.	The health & condition of the horses of the Division continues satisfactory. The 4th Bde R.H.A. with Ammunition Column, returned to the Divn. on the 24th inst, with a proportion of their horses in somewhat poor condition, particularly C. Battery — they had been picketed out & exposed to all weathers and had not been clipped — under instructions from D.V.S. horses have been shod with metal strips made from biscuit-tin inserted under the shoes, another trial to reduce the number of injuries due to picked up nails. G.O.C. of the 4th Bde Arty does not find favour with the Regtl. of one Brigade only visiting the extra labour & it is very difficult to get sufficient movement of the 37 horses have been evacuated from the Divn during the month — of these 6 have been for mange; 5 for "inability to withstand the rigourous surgical conditions".	

G.H. Pridge 2 Major ADVS
3rd Cav. Divn

ADVS

Army Form C. 2118.

WAR DIARY
or
INTELLIGENCE SUMMARY.
(Erase heading not required.)

Place	Date	Hour	Summary of Events and Information	Remarks and references to Appendices
TREPIED	31/12/16		Health & condition of horses of 3rd Cav. Div. satisfactory - Mange has been somewhat prevalent during the month - particularly in "C" Sqdn of 3rd D.G's. in which it started at AIRON-NOTRE-DAME. The 6th & 8th Cav. Bdes reclaufs areas during the month. "D" Sqdn of 10 Hussars moving into AIRON NOTRE-DAME. They only stay there however for about 8 nights & then move to billets near BERCK so minimising the risk of their contracting mange. This disease being very prevalent amongst civilian horses in the AIRON-NOTRE DAME & A. St. VAAST areas. In a farm at the latter village, where a Sqdn of the Blues are billetted, 5 out of 11 farm there are badly affected & cart are being made for them twice a Sqdn of the Blues. our efforts are being made for them twice to another locality. There is little done that the cases in the 3rd D.G's started on an infection from some civilian source. - 118 horses have been evacuated from the Divn during the month of which 60 have been for debility & 25 for mange or suspected mange of this 25 - 17 have been from the 3rd D.G's - No cases of Pthisis & need have been heard also during the month. C.H. Jeffreys. Maj AVC. ADVS 3rd Cav Div.	ADVS 31/12/16

WAR DIARY
or
INTELLIGENCE SUMMARY.
(Erase heading not required)

ADVS 3Cav(D)
Vol/13

Place	Date	Hour	Summary of Events and Information	Remarks and references to Appendices
TREPIED	31/1/17		3rd Cav Divn. Health & condition of horses of the Divn have been normal during the month of January — 95 have been evacuated of which 15 have been for Mange or suspected mange & 37 for debility — of the latter most of them have had some additional disease or disability — such as mange or chronic coughs — On Thurs. 1. Feby. the 7th & 8th B'des are to exchange areas — the 6th B'de remaining as before — 7th is reported that the locality where 2 Squadrons of 2nd Life G'ds are to be billetted (viz; GROFFLIERS, LA FOLIE & LA SANTÉ FARMS) will have to be vacated, and that their squadrons will have to go to AIRON-ST-VAAST & A. NOTRE-DAME. where mange is known to be prevalent amongst the French Cavalry horses. I have reported to Brigades H.Q. that this will constitute a serious risk of infection to the horses of these B'gdes — A dipping bath Calcium Sulphide for all horses of the Divn is in course of construction at NEUFVILLE, North of MONTREUIL, and it is hoped that it will be finished within the next fortnight or so —	

{signature} Maj. A.V.C.
A.D.V.S.
3rd Cav. Divn.

WAR DIARY
or
INTELLIGENCE SUMMARY
(Erase heading not required.)

Army Form C. 2118.

Place	Date	Hour	Summary of Events and Information	Remarks and references to Appendices
TREPIED	28.2.17		Health & condition of horses of 3rd Cav. Div. continues satisfactory. — Orders were received on the 3rd inst. ult. from D.D.V.S. Cav. Corps that owing to congestion at Veterinary Hospitals no horses (Veterinary cases) were to be evacuated till further orders, which have not except hard record. Mange continues up to the present well under control — there are however one or two cases in each of the following: — 5th Cav. Reserve Park; N. Somerset Yeo; 8th M.G. Squadron; 10th Hussars; Leicester Yeo; Essex Yeomy. There has been no contagious or contagious of ailments in the 3rd D.G.b which has been almost recovered and all are another one in E. Squadron of the Essex or from. —	

Capt Duff. maj A.D.V.S. 3rd Cav Div

WAR DIARY
or
INTELLIGENCE SUMMARY.

Army Form C. 2118.

ANZAC 3 Cav Bde

Place	Date	Hour	Summary of Events and Information	Remarks and references to Appendices
TREFIED	31-3-17		Health & condition of horses of 3rd Cav. Divn. continues satisfactory. Remounts on the 20th inst., in consequence of welding being eased for the previous 6-7 weeks, up to the [illegible] end of the month. Of those 10 horses were evacuated to the [illegible] sick [illegible], as 18 of debility [illegible] cases of mange, so of debility [illegible] change. The [illegible] mange out has not been in use. I found that badly when finished, and it became necessary to relay the whole of [illegible] [illegible] in consequence of which it is not yet ready for use.	

Comdg 9[?] Maj AVC,
3rd Cav Divn.

Army Form C. 2118.

WAR DIARY
or
INTELLIGENCE SUMMARY.

(Erase heading not required.)

A.D.V.S. 3rd Cav Divn

1 - 30 April 1917

Place	Date	Hour	Summary of Events and Information	Remarks and references to Appendices
LIENCOURT	30/4/17		On the 5th inst., the Division left the Winter area & proceeded towards ARRAS & on the 9th, 10th, & 11th went into section between ARRAS & MONCHY-LE-PREUX the 7th Cav. Bde being in reserve. As a result of this there were about 1100 horse-casualties killed, wounded, missing & evacuated. A copy of my report to D.D.V.S. Cav Corps on the very onerous duties during these operations, is appended hereto. There appears to be a great deal of difficulty in obtaining accurate figures of horse casualties — Units themselves, not knowing till some days later what was the number of casualties — & in a large proportion of cases it was quite impossible to find out what has become of the horses that were missing — This would appear to me to be a difficulty that is always likely to arise under circumstances such as those which occurred. The only way to arrive at figures which would be anywhere approaching accurate would be to call every Unit to produce — its own surviving men — wounded or otherwise — as to what became of his horse in which would be a lengthy process — moreover it would still leave a huge gap of "missing & untraceable" — for the reason that what happens in this last action is liable to happen in every other action.	V/1/16

WAR DIARY or INTELLIGENCE SUMMARY

Army Form C. 2118.

(Erase heading not required.)

Place	Date	Hour	Summary of Events and Information	Remarks and references to Appendices

HQ's for fear of horseholders to be severly & continually shelled, with the result that men & horses are killed & wounded, over the remainder of the horses - wounded & unwounded stampede to the troops, some dying of exhaustion, wounds of injuries, some being shot destroyed by unknown which also who turn them on the road. Some being caught & either returned or evacuated by unknown units, others straying to farms & will(?) yrs(?) bringdown. Have either returns or go(?) let by the inhabitants - This is bound to happen however had the V.O.s & M.V.Os there may work to prevent it - There is also another source of loss that will be unaccounted for these i.e. the horses of men who have been killed or died of wounds, or so seriously wounded to be able to answer questions.

On April 13th the Division bithdraw(?) from the front. Considering the frightful weather that prevailed during the time that the Div'n was in action, the hard unbroken condition of the horses, & their forced condition being only(?) sub(?) nose- & drawing civilian oats(?) bought from the farms at increased ration 12# Oats + 12# of Hay & 2# of bran, with an additional 2# of Oats for horses of the Household Cavy. & th 16 Lancers.

C.H.Blofelt(?). Maj. O.D.V.S.
3rd Cav: Div'n.

2353 Wt. W2344/1454 700,000 5/15 D.D. & L.   A.D.S.S./Forms/C. 2118.

Copy

D.D.V.S
Cav. Corps

In compliance with your instructions I beg to forward the following remarks on the recent Cavalry operations -

On April 8th the 3 M.V Sections became "Divisionalized". The 'A' Echelons were also Divisionalized and divided into 'A1' and 'A2's. 'B' Echelon remained at BOUBERS-SUR-CANCHE (3 miles West of FREVENT) when the Division moved from that area on the morning of April 8th and the 3 M.V.S's followed the A2 Echelon to the concentration point (GOUY-EN-ARTOIS). On April 9th the Bdes received orders to advance towards ARRAS & about midday the A Echelons proceeded to follow the Bdes. The leading Bde was to march to a point - C13, d 9.6 Map S1B 1/40,000. Having no idea how far beyond this point the Bdes might proceed, I left the 20th M.V.S at GOUY-EN-ARTOIS, as the rear Section, whilst the 13th & 14th M.V.S's followed the A Echelon, and finally halted late on the night of Apr. 9th at a point 1 mile East of DUISANS. On the evening of April 10th, the Bdes were ordered to advance East of ARRAS, the A Echelon to follow them. The 13th M.V.S then proceeded with A Echelon, and halted near ARRAS station, the 14th remaining where it was, 1 mile East of DUISANS, to act as the link between the forward 13th Section and the rearward 20th Section.

On April 11th there were 36 horses at the 14th M.V.S awaiting evacuation - some of which had been sent back from the 13th Section. Arrangements were made for these to be evacuated from AGNEZ. On this date I was on the point of ordering the 20th M.V.S to come up to DUISANS, and of sending the 14th on to ARRAS, when I received information that the Divn had been ordered back. The Bdes reached the DUISANS - ARRAS Road during the night of Apr 11th & early morning of April 12th, and halted there till about 8 a.m. of the 12th, when they proceeded back to GOUY-EN-ARTOIS. The 13th M.V.S remained in ARRAS and on the 12th, 13th & 14th, the O.C. (Capt ELLISON) was out with a party between ARRAS and MONCHY-LE-PREUX searching for loose and

(Continued)

wounded horses. During this period the 14th M.V.S. remained at the same position, 1 mile East of DUISANS, awaiting trucks wherewith to evacuate from AGNEZ between 90 & 100 sick & wounded horses which had been collected at his section. It would have been useless to send these horses back to the 20th Section at GOUY- for one thing there would have been the same delay in obtaining trucks at GOUY-EN-ARTOIS as was the case at AGNEZ, and for another thing the condition of the horses was such that one desired to subject them to the barest minimum of road travelling.

I think it would have been better as things turned out if I had brought the 20th Section up to DUISANS on the 9th, with the other 2 Sections, and on the evening of the 10th, the 13th & 14th sections should both have gone on to ARRAS, the 20th remaining East of DUISANS and on the 11th - one of these Sections - or at any rate a party from one of them, should have proceeded in rear of the 2 forward Bdes and left A.Echelon behind them and gone on to the A.P.M's. collecting post, and there co-operated with the Bde. V.O's., in collecting &c stray or wounded horses.

I was undoubtedly too far back to be able to keep in touch with the Bdes' operations which last factor is a necessity for an A.D.V.S., to enable him to post his M.V. Sections in the most useful positions, but the position I took was that which had been assigned to me under the written instructions from Divisional G.S.-

(Sgd) C. H. H. JOLLIFFE, Major, A.V.C.
A.D.V.S. 3rd Cavalry Division

16/4/17

It will be seen from the above that it would have been perfectly useless to have ever thought of leaving a section with the 'B' Echelon.

WAR DIARY
or
INTELLIGENCE SUMMARY.

Army Form C. 2118.

ADVS 3 Cav D

Place	Date	Hour	Summary of Events and Information	Remarks and references to Appendices
FLAMICOURT	1st to 31st May. 1917		On the 13th inst. the DuSR kept the previous area, and reached its present area on the 19th, for the purpose of looking after the of the Div, 3 Bdes being in the line and one back in reserve. While Bdes are in the line there is only one van [?] to attend to each, but in spite of this the horses are up to the present time all in very good condition. There is excellent & copious grazing, of which full advantage is being taken, in consequence of which the hours have all but in a considerable amount of flesh. They may have to be somewhat "soft" immediately, but to any extent more or at the termination of the present phase of the DuSR looking after Div –	

Cpt [signature] Maj. a.v.c.
ADVS 3rd Cav. Div

Total number of horses evacuated during this month was 130 + 5 mules. Of these 36 were evacuated for Debility, 9 for Mange, + 7 for Ulcerative Lolulities.

Army Form C. 2118.

WAR DIARY
or
INTELLIGENCE SUMMARY.
(Erase heading not required.)

ADVS 3 Cav D

1st to 30th June 1917.   WS 8/8

Place	Date	Hour	Summary of Events and Information	Remarks and references to Appendices
FLAMECOURT	30 June 1917.		The horses of the 3rd Cav. Div. are all in very good condition through possibly somewhat soft, but 6 any sudden heavy work – for the past month they have been doing practically nothing except grazing & light exercise – The weather if exceptional does not however show any material decrease during the month. 129 heads & 5 mules having been evacuated – of these 19 were for mange and 8 for debility & the remaining 107 for various causes – such as chronic lameness, sore backs & barbed wire wounds. There being a large amount of barbed wire round this district –	

Cantliffe Major
a/ADVS
3rd Cav. Div.

WAR DIARY
or
INTELLIGENCE SUMMARY.

Army Form C. 2118.

D ADVS Vol II 19

Place	Date	Hour	Summary of Events and Information	Remarks and references to Appendices
BUSNES.	21 July 1917.		Health & condition of horses of 3rd Cav. Divn. continues satisfactory, though as a whole they are carrying less flesh than was the case a month ago. During the latter half of May and the whole of June while the horses were in the PERONNE, TINCOURT, VILLERS FAUCON Area they had a very large amount of grazing. They left that area on the 2nd & 3rd of July. Since then they have had practically no grazing at all, & some loss of flesh has resulted. — 105 animals have been evacuated from the Divn during the month, of which 73 were for Debility. — Besides these, 18 animals of Units not belonging to the 3rd Cav. Divn. were evacuated by M.V. Sects of this Divn.	

Crookshank, Major,
A.D.V.S.
3rd Cav. Divn.

WAR DIARY
or
INTELLIGENCE SUMMARY.

Army Form C. 2118.

ADVS 3rd Cavalry Div.

1 – 31 Aug. 1917.

Place	Date	Hour	Summary of Events and Information	Remarks and references to Appendices
RUSMES	31-8-17		Health & condition of horses of 3rd Cav. Div. continues satisfactory. 79 horses have been evacuated for vety. reasons during the month — of these 8 have been on account of mange; 13 on account of debility, 25 12 on account of debility combined with some abnormal sickness or injury. In addition to these, 29 horses from Units outside this Div. with have been evacuated by M.V. by cases of this Div. – of the latter, 6 horse from for Mange & 5 for Debility.	

Capt. Blythe, Maj. AVC.
ADVS
3rd Cav. Div.

Army Form C. 2118.

A.S.V. 5. 3rd Cavalry Division

WAR DIARY
INTELLIGENCE SUMMARY.
(Erase heading not required.)

Instructions regarding War Diaries and Intelligence Summaries are contained in F.S. Regs., Part II. and the Staff Manual respectively. Title pages will be prepared in manuscript.

Place	Date	Hour	Summary of Events and Information	Remarks and references to Appendices
BUSNES	1-30. Sept. 1917			
	30.9.17		Health & condition of troops of 3rd Cav. Divn on whole satisfactory. 101 horses have been evacuated from the Divn for Veterinary reasons, of which 6 have been on account of Mange and 26 for debility. In addition to these 43 have belonged to other formations have also been evacuated from M.V. Section of this Divn.	

Capt Phipps, Major AVC
A.D.V.S.
3rd Cav. Divn

WAR DIARY

Army Form C. 2118.

A.D.V.S. 3rd Cavalry Division

INTELLIGENCE SUMMARY

(Erase heading not required.)

Place	Date	Hour	Summary of Events and Information	Remarks and references to Appendices
DOMART EN PONTHIEU	31/10/17		Health & condition of horses of 8th Bde Cav. Div. us. continues satisfactory. 186 animals have been evacuated from the Div. during the month for vety. reasons - of these 5 only have been evacuated on account of mange, and 17 on a/c of debility. In addition 160 animals from units of other formations outside this Div. have been evacuated by M.V. Section of this Div.	

Capt AVC Maj
a.d.v.s
3rd Cav Div

[stamp: A.D.V.S. 3rd CAVALRY DIVISION 10/11/17]

WAR DIARY or INTELLIGENCE SUMMARY

Army Form C. 2118.

ADV 3 3 Cav 9/12/35

Place	Date	Hour	Summary of Events and Information	Remarks and references to Appendices
CORBIE	9 Dec 17		Health — condition of horses of 3rd Cav Div. is satisfactory, except for the forward Brigade's Lympthangitis in the 2nd Life Guards. Two cases were first discovered in horses evacuated to No 22 V.H. on 12-11-17. Since then there have been an additional 90 cases, full reports have been sent to DDVS Cav Corps. 191 animals (187 horses & 4 mules) have been evacuated during month of November. Of these 80 were evacuated for debility, 19 for mange & for Epiz. Lymphangitis, instructed by D.V.S. 3rd Army & sent by him to be of actually warranted no 54 Epiz Lymph. Si Contacts. The remainder were miscellaneous and shows — mostly lameness. Besides these, 12 animals of other formations were evacuated by M.V. Secns of this Div.	

CHMcliffe Maj.
ADVS
3rd Cav Div.

WAR DIARY or INTELLIGENCE SUMMARY

Army Form C. 2118.

Place: DOMART-EN-PONTHIEU
Date: 31. Dec. 1917.

Sporadic lymphangitis continues to occur in 2nd Life Gds — there having been 9 to 9 a.m. (date of last war diary) — 9 cases since.

The disease appears to be so far confined entirely to that Regt. No cases having been discovered in any other Unit, though smears have been taken & examined at No 5 V.H. from horses of 1st Life Gds, R.H.Gds, & 7th Bde, which have shown abrasions of slightly virulent character, & a negative result reported. Questionable failure in connection with the majority of these cases in the 2nd Life Gds has been that there was no perceptible enlargement of lymphatic glands of corrupt lymphatic vessels, although lymphoccci were found to be present in smears taken from lesions that merely had the appearance in many cases of simple abrasions, which would seem to show that lymphatics and ?? of the disease later in the earlier stages of the disease.

Apart from this lymphangitis the health & condition of horses of the [3rd?] Cavalry Division...

Army Form C. 2118.

WAR DIARY
or
INTELLIGENCE SUMMARY.
(Erase heading not required.)

Place	Date	Hour	Summary of Events and Information	Remarks and references to Appendices
	1-31. Dec.'17 (contd)		The Div'n is satisfactory. 93 animals have been evacuated from the Div during the month, of which 26 were to have been for mange & 5 for debility and 3 to 2 Vet Gen Hosp after injurious wounds received later. The remainder various —	

C.H. Bayliff
Maj. AVC.
ADVS. 3rd Cav Div.

WAR DIARY
or
INTELLIGENCE SUMMARY.
(Erase heading not required.)

Army Form C. 2118.

WO95/3525

Place	Date	Hour	Summary of Events and Information	Remarks and references to Appendices
MONCHY LACACHE	31-1-18.		Health & condition of horses of 3rd Cav Bde W.R. is satisfactory. The 2nd tip Gds. which had a outbreak of Strang: on the Sympathetic tie left the B.W.R. & went to L of C. area, in its place & both coy of the 2nd V.H. from 2nd B.W.R. — Since when there have been no further cases in the B.W.R. — except one which was sent up from a B.W.R. on a charge for Lt Stanley Rtt Gds. This cat was immediately destroyed by R.S.C. by Rtt Col. SMITH. Pt. C.O.V.S. destroyed. 123 animals have been evacuated from the Du.S. 21 during the month of January. 57 Vans for mange. 14 for mainly + H. "E.L." Conducts, in conjunction with the Veterinary adventures — in addition 3 animals of other formations were evacuated by M.V. Sadrns of this Div.	

C. Ralph Maj. O.V.S.
a.D.V.S.
3rd Cav Div.

WAR DIARY
or
INTELLIGENCE SUMMARY.

(Erase heading not required.)

Army Form C/2118.

Place	Date	Hour	Summary of Events and Information	Remarks and references to Appendices
MONCHY LAGACHE	28.2.18		Health & condition of horses of 32nd Coy DWR satisfactory – 75 animals have been evacuated to Army Veterinary Sections during month of which 11 were for Debility, 5 for wounds, in addition to these a further 57 animals from Units of other formations have been evacuated from M.V.S. Cases of Epithelium contagiosa continues important – Catarrhal May are	Capt. V.S. 32nd Coy DWR

WAR DIARY
INTELLIGENCE SUMMARY

ADV V S⁸ Cav R⁹M

Place	Date	Hour	Summary of Events and Information	Remarks and references to Appendices
RIVERY) AMIENS	1-31. March 1918.	9.4.18	During month of March 1918, 174 animals of 3ᵈ Cav. Bde were evacuated for veterinary treatment. Of these, 22 went for mange, 25 for debility & 83 for battle wounds. Besides these, H/animals of other formations were evacuated by M.V.Section of 3ᵈ Cav. Div.	
			Horse Lt Col Carey left the Divⁿ on 9.3.18, Lt 17 Lt Lancers, 6 Gn. Dragoons and 7th D.G.'s taking on same date Base, Reinforcement & N Service Veterinary & 20th M.V.S. Cpl/15 Divⁿ on 14-3-18. The Canadian Cav Regts took their places the same day.	
			Ref A.G.'s Office at the Base, see Section No 17/259/18 of 19-3-18. The 3ᵈ Cav Div disembarked in Belgium 8.10.14. Herewith a copy of report to 8th V S Cav Corps on receipt of re action	

Crampelap. Maj
ADV S 3ᵈ Cav Div

WAR DIARY
or
INTELLIGENCE SUMMARY.
(Erase heading not required.)

Army Form C. 2118.

BAYS & Cav D

1st to 30th April 1918.

Place	Date	Hour	Summary of Events and Information	Remarks and references to Appendices
PERNES	30.4.18		Health & condition of horses of 3rd Cav Dn. have been satisfactory during the month of April. — 409 animals have been evacuated from the Divn. during the month. Of these 8 were for ulcerative lymphitis, 9 for mange, 100 for debility, 16 for ophthalmia, and 95 for wounds & gunshot, the remaining 181 being from various causes, mostly lameness & wounds & sore.	

Cuff cliffe Major.
O/C A.V.S.
3rd Cav. Dn.

Extract from Weekly Technical Report for W/E. 4-4-'18

Condition of horses has undoubtedly fallen off in consequence of conditions prevailing during the past fortnight entailing during the first week long marches and hard work, and during the second week long hours without being off-saddled, continuous exposure to inclement weather, irregular and often insufficient watering and feeding. In consequence of this a large proportion of horses are looking thin and "tucked up", but I am of opinion that a period of rest and normal routine will soon effect a marked improvement in the general condition of the horses.

In consequence of the uncertainty of our movements or operations from one hour to the next, M.V. Sections remained with their Brigades till April 1st., when they were "Divisionalised". On this date (Reference Amiens Map 1/100,000) Divl. H.Q. moved in the early morning to BOVES (2E.) and 6th & 7th Cav. Bdes. were concentrated in BOIS DE GENTELLES (2E) the 13th & 14th M.V. Sections being placed at the N.W. Corner of BOIS DE BOVES (2E) to await orders.

[The Canadian Cavalry Brigade was then detached from the Division & was with the 2nd Cavalry Division, having gone to them on the 27th March, the Canadian M.V. Section accompanying them.]

On April 1st, as soon as orders were given for the 6th Cav. Bde. to advance from BOIS DE GENTELLES, the 13th M.V.S. was sent forward to follow them and get in touch with the Brigade Commander, and to send back any ineffective horses to 14th M.V.S. which remained at N.W. Corner of BOIS DE BOVES.

On April 2nd. Divl. H.Q. moved to BLANGY TRONVILLE, the 14th M.V.S. going from BOIS DE BOVES to same village. 7th Cav. Bde. moved to wood "100", 2 Kilometres due South of Church of BLANGY TRONVILLE, where it was joined by the 6th Cav. Bde. which had the previous day advanced from the BOIS DE GENTELLES, the 13th M.V.S. returning at the same time to BLANGY TRONVILLE so that on the night 2nd/3rd April both M.V.S's were in this village, the 14th M.V.S. having that day evacuated 12 animals by rail from SALEUX (2C)

On April 3rd, the 6th Cav Bde went into action between FOUILLOY (2G) & VILLERS BRETONNEUX. The 13th M.V.S. moved from BLANGY TRONVILLE to FOUILLOY Village, the C.O. going forward during the day with 6 men to keep in touch with 6th Cav Bde. H.Q. and form a Veterinary Collecting Post, in conjunction with the Regimental V.Os. of that Brigade. On same day the 14th M.V.S. evacuated another 29 horses by rail from SALEUX, of which 11 had been sent back from the 13th M.V.S. to the 14th M.V.S.

On April 4th, the 6th & 7th Cav. Bdes. were both in action. The 13th M.V.S. formed a Veterinary Collecting Post in touch with 6th Cav. Bde. and O.C., 14th M.V.S. went up with a party of 8 men from BLANGY TRONVILLE and formed a Veterinary Collecting Post in touch with the 7th Cav Bde. About 40 animals were collected. During night of April 4th/5th the horses were sent back, the Brigades holding the line, dismounted, and the Veterinary Collecting Posts were accordingly withdrawn during the early hours of April 4th the party from

13th M.V.S. returning to FOUILLOY where it rejoined the rest of the Section & proceeded to Wood "100" (above mentioned on reverse). Where the horses of the 2 Brigades had been sent to.

On April 5th the horses had a rest, the 6th & 7th Cav. Bdes. continuing to hold the line dismounted and on this date 67 horses were evacuated by the 13th & 14th M.V. Sections which was done by sending them to the Canadian M.V.S. which had rejoined the Division on the 3rd inst. and proceeded on the 4th inst. to CAMON (Q.E.) to which place these horses for evacuation were sent.

On April 6th the Division moved to the present locations and on that date I saw OC, Canadian M.V.S. and learnt that he had established a Veterinary Evacuation Station at SALEUX, having obtained P.B. men from his Brigade to act as train-conducting parties.

As will be seen from the above, all evacuations from this Division (as well I believe, as from 2nd Cavalry Division) have been carried out from SALEUX - which has proved a most useful station. The Veterinary Evacuation Station at PICQUIGNY has been perfectly useless so far as this Division is concerned, being much too far back for horses to be sent there - nearly 18 miles from the scene of operations.

CH Hyslop, Maj.
ADVS
3rd C.D.

ADVS 3 Cav Dn

No. 29

WAR DIARY
or
INTELLIGENCE SUMMARY.

Army Form C. 2118.

(Erase heading not required.)

Place	Date	Hour	Summary of Events and Information	Remarks and references to Appendices
YZEUX	31/5/18		1st to 31st May 1918 Health & condition of horses of 3rd Cavalry Division have been satisfactory during the month of May. 295 animals have been evacuated from the Division during the month, of these 4 were for Mange, 84 for Debility, 22 for Ophthalmia, 3 for Ulcerative Cellulitis, and 11 for Wounds &c. The remaining 146 were being from various causes mostly lameness and injuries &c. Besides these 41 animals of other formations were evacuated by Mobile Veterinary Sections of this Division.	

C.H.K.Sugg?
Major, AVC
AVS, 3rd Cavalry Division

WAR DIARY
or
INTELLIGENCE SUMMARY.

Army Form C. 2118.

ADVS 3 Cav Div
Vol 1

1st to 30th JUNE 1918

Place	Date	Hour	Summary of Events and Information	Remarks and references to Appendices
YZEUX	16th June	—	Major C.H.H. SCHLIFFE, Arr. proceeded for duty as D.A.D.V.S. HQ., L. of C. Sinstram 16-6-18	
			Joined 3rd Cav Division for duty as ADVS.	
	17th	"	Visited HQ 6th Cav Bde, Royal Dragoons + 13th VS.	
	18th	"	Visited A.H.T.Coy. Canadian Cavalry Brigade + 3rd Signal Sqdn.	
	19th	"	Office Routine	
	20th	"	Inspected Canadian Cavalry Brigade	
	21st	"	Visited 3 Cavalry Regiments of 6th Cav Bde. with 1st Brig. General 7th Cav Bde	
	22nd	"	D.D.V.S. Cavalry Corps came over. Visited 13th M.V.S. + H.Q. A.S.C.	
	23rd	"	Inspected animals of 3rd Cav Reserve Park + Army H.T. Coy	
	24th	"	Inspected animals of C Battery R.H.A. + HQ 4th Bde R.H.A.	
	25th	"	Visited 14th M.V.S. HQ 7th Cav Bde.	
	26th	"	Visited HQ 6th Cav Bde.	
	27th	"	Inspected animals of K Battery R.H.A. D.A. Column & 7th Cav S. 7th Cav Bde H.Q.	
			14th M.V.S. + 7th Signal troop	
	28th	"	Inspected animals of 3rd Dragoon Guards, Royal Dragoons, 10th Royal Hussars	
	29th	"	Inspected animals of 7th Dragoon Guards, 17th Lancers + Inniskill. Dragoons	
	30th	"	Inspected animals of H.Q. 3rd Cavalry Division	

W. Clarke Lieut-Colonel
ADVS 3rd Cavalry Division

3rd Cavalry Divn
Army Form C. 2118.

WAR DIARY
or
INTELLIGENCE SUMMARY
(Erase heading not required.)

Vol 31

Page 1 July 1st to 31st 1918

Place	Date	Hour	Summary of Events and Information	Remarks and references to Appendices
YZEUX	1st July		Inspected 6th M.G. Sqdn	
	2nd "		Inspected 3rd Field Sqdn RE	
	3rd "		Inspected 6th C.F.A	
	4th "		" 14th M.V. Section	
	5th "		" 3rd Signal Sqdn R.E. & Hydro. horse	
	6th "		Official visit to 14th Veterinary Hospital	
	7th "		Inspected HQ. Can. Cav. Bde. A'Can M.V Section & 13th M.V.S	
	8th "		" Fort Garry Horse	
	9th "		" Royal Canadian Dragoons & Canadian Signal Troop	
	10th "		" Lord Strathcona's Horse	
	11th "		" 6th Inniskilling Dragoons	
	12th "		" Canadian M.G. Sqdn	
	13th "		" 3rd Signal Sqdn R.E. & H.Q. A.S.C	
	14th "		" 3rd Cav. Reserve Regt. & Aux. H.T. Coy.	
	15th "		Office Routine	
	16th "		Inspected 7th Dragoon Guards and 17th Lancers	

W.D.
3rd Cavalry Div.

Army Form C. 2118.

WAR DIARY
or
INTELLIGENCE SUMMARY
(Erase heading not required.)

Page 2

Instructions regarding War Diaries and Intelligence Summaries are contained in F. S. Regs., Part II. and the Staff Manual respectively. Title pages will be prepared in manuscript.

Place	Date	Hour	Summary of Events and Information	Remarks and references to Appendices
YZEUX	17th July		(Continued)	
	18th		Inspected 3rd Dragoon Guards and 1st Royal Dragoons	
			" 10th Royal Hussars and 6th G. Squadron	
	19th		" 7th M.G. Sqdn and 7th C.F. Ambulance	
	20th		Office Routine	
	21st		Conference of Veterinary Officers	
	22nd		Visited 13th M.V. Section, H.Q. 6th Cav Bde. H.Q. Canadian Cavalry Brigade	
	23rd		Inspected S.A.A. Section, Div Amm Col. + H.Q. 7 Cav Bde.	
			14th M.V. Section	
	24th		H.Q. M.V.S. Can C.F.A. + H.Q. Can Cav Bde	
	25th		Inspected 6th C.F. Ambulance	
			" H.Q. 7th Cav Bde. 14th M.V. Section + Div Amm Col.	
	26th		Visited & inside of 7th Cav Bde with AA + QMG	
	27th		" H.Q. 6th Cav Bde + 13th M.V.S.	
	28th		" H.Q. 6th Cav Bde Canadian M.V. Section Canadian Signal Troop	
			Canadian C.F. Amb. Fort Garry Horse	
	29th		Inspected H.Q. 7th Cav Bde, 14th M.V.S. + 7th Signal Troop	
	30th		Visited 7th Cav Bde. Tactical Scheme + 6th Cav Bde Horse Show	

Army Form C. 2118.

WAR DIARY
or
INTELLIGENCE SUMMARY.
(Erase heading not required.)

Page 3

Place	Date	Hour	Summary of Events and Information	Remarks and references to Appendices
YZEUX	30 July		Continued Office Routine	

A.D.V.S.
Date 7/8/18
3rd CAVALRY DIVISION

O. Curtis
Lieut-Colonel
A.D.V.S., 3rd Cavalry Division

Army Form C. 2118.

A.D.V.S., 3rd Cavalry Division

WAR DIARY
INTELLIGENCE SUMMARY.
(Erase heading not required.)

16

Title pages 1st – 31st August 1918

Place	Date	Hour	Summary of Events and Information	Remarks and references to Appendices
YZEUX	August 1st		Inspected 3rd Field Squadron R.E.	
	2nd		"C" and "K" Batteries R.H.A. were inspected and also Amm: Col. of "Bois" R.H.A. "A" + "B" Batteries R.C.H.A. + Amm: Col. of C.H.A Bde in Daily Mail Wood	
	3rd		Visited A.D.V.S. III Corps. Visited H.Q., 6th Cav. Bde, 10th Royal Hussars, Royal Canadian Dragoons and Canadian M.G. Sqdn.	
	4th		Office Routine.	
	5th		Attended conference at Divnl HQ at 9 am. Visited A.D.V.S. Canadian Corps, D.D.V.S. Fourth Army, 6th Inniskilling Dragoons	
	6th		Visited Canadian Cavalry Brigade, Y? Cavalry Brigade + 14th Mobile Vety Section	
PONT de METZ	7th		Proceeded to PONT de METZ and Divl. H.Q. Arrived at the Chau. at Pont de Metz. The 3 M.V. Sections became Divisional.	
	8th		13th M.V.S. moved to SALEUX. Hostilities commenced this day. Left with 14th April "A" Cav M.V.S's at 3 a.m. The 14th M.V.S. marched to BOVES and "A" Cdn M.V.S. to N.W. corner of BOIS de GENTELLES 4 hours after Zero time and took the same along as the HOURGES (Domart sur Luce).	
	9th		A. Cdn. M.V.S. moved up to Ignaucourt, the palace at Hourges being taken over by	

Army Form C. 2118.

WAR DIARY
or
INTELLIGENCE SUMMARY.
(Erase heading not required.)

Instructions regarding War Diaries and Intelligence Summaries are contained in F. S. Regs., Part II. and the Staff Manual respectively. Title pages will be prepared in manuscript.

Place	Date	Hour	Summary of Events and Information	Remarks and references to Appendices
	1st to 31st August			
	August 7th		The 14th M.V.S. from BOVES. The 13th M.V.S. with up the position of 4/7/7's at BOVES.	
	August 10th		"A" Coln M.V.S. moved up to Corie, the 14th & 13th M.V.S. remaining in the same position.	
	" 11th		Location of M.V.S's remained the same. Evacuation of the 11th Division moved to BOVES	
	" 12th		Divisional HdQrs at BOIS de BOVES. "A" Coln M.V.S. rejoined its Brigade at Le PARRAQUET.	
	" 13th		Divisional HdQrs moved to SAINS en AMIENOIS. 13th & 14th M.V. Sections rejoined their Brigades.	
	" 14th		Brid. HdQrs at SAINS en AMIENOIS. Conference of Veterinary Officers under R.Royal Dragoons and R.C. Machine Gun Sqdn.	
	" 15th		Visited HQ Canadian Cavalry Brigade. "A" Coln M.V.S. and Royal Canadian Dragoons.	
			Divisional HdQrs moved to YZEUX.	
	" 16th		Visit from D.D.V.S., Cavalry Corps and Lt.Col. Gray	
	" 17th		Conference at Brid. HdQrs + Office routine	
	" 18th		Acted as Judge a/c a Shoeing Competition in the 14th Lancers.	
	" 19th		Visited HQ Canadian Cavalry Brigade, Lord Strathcona Horse "A" Coln M.V.S. "A" Batty R.C.H.A.	

Army Form C. 2118.

WAR DIARY
INTELLIGENCE SUMMARY
(Erase heading not required.)

Instructions regarding War Diaries and Intelligence Summaries are contained in F. S. Regs., Part II. and the Staff Manual respectively. Title pages will be prepared in manuscript.

Place	Date	Hour	Summary of Events and Information	Remarks and references to Appendices
YZEUX	August 20th		1st to 31st August.	
			Inspected Fort Gay Horse.	
	21st		Standing To. Office Routine	
	22nd		Visited H.Qrs Canadian Cavalry Brigade, 13th, 14th & A Cdn M.V. Section. with D.D.V.S. Cavalry Corps.	
	23rd		Standing To. Office Routine	
	24th		do	
	25th		Moved to Fontaine L'Etalon	
Fontaine L'Etalon	26th		Moved to Ward [?] 3rd Field [?] & Light Section 3rd Cavalry Reserve Park	
			Visited 3rd Field Squadron R.E. and Light Section 3rd Cavalry Reserve Park.	
WAIL	27th		Visited Canadian Cavalry Brigade H.Q. 7th Cavalry Brigade H.Q. & 14th M.V. Section	
	28th		Visited Ht Bde R.C.H.A Ammn Col. and R.C.H.A Bde Ammn Col.	
	29th		Visited B. Echelon.	
	30th		Visited H.Q. B. Cav Bde, and H.Q. Canadian Cavalry Brigade and 13th M.V. Section	
	31st		Visited R.C.H.A Bde Ammn Column, 14th Veterinary Hospital ABBEVILLE, No 2 Stationary Hospital ABBEVILLE and D.D.V.S Cavalry Corps.	

O. Cluff
Lieut Colonel
A.D.V.S, 3rd Cavalry Division

ADV83 Cav Corps

9823

WAR DIARY
or
INTELLIGENCE SUMMARY.
(Erase heading not required.)

Army Form C. 2118.

September 1918

Place	Date	Hour	Summary of Events and Information	Remarks and references to Appendices
Wailly	Sept 1st		Visited D.V.S. Neuchatel	
"	2nd		Office routine	
"	3rd		Visited G.H.T. Coy. Heavy Section Reserve Park. Visit from D.D.V.S Cdn Corps.	
"	4th		Visited 13th – 14th, A.Cav. M.V.S. – Canadian Cav. Bde.	
"	5th		Visited Canadian M. V.S. & Fd. Army Horse	
"	6th		Left for Dieppe	
"	7th to 21st		From – to U.K.	
Fontaine	22nd		Pyramid Divisim	
L'Etalon	23rd		Inspection of V.O.s of Canadian Cavalry Brigade trams. Visit from D.D.V.S. A Corps	
"	24th		Visited 6 AT Coy. 6th & 7th Pack Hzys. 13th & 14th M.V.S.	
"	25th		Visited Cattle Isolation. A.H.T Coy. – Left for Maricourt	
Maricourt	26th		Visited 7th & 8th.	
Maricourt	27th		Left for Clery	
Clery	28th		Conference with V.Os.	
"	29th		Left for Poreilly	
Poreilly	30th		Poreilly Office routine.	

A 6945 Wt. W14422/M160 330,000 12/16 D.D. & L. Forms/C./2118/14.

A Crosby
H/Colonel
ADVS 3rd Cav Division
7/10/18

WAR DIARY
INTELLIGENCE SUMMARY

Army Form C. 2118.

(Erase heading not required.)

Place	Date	Hour	Summary of Events and Information	Remarks and references to Appendices
POUILLY	Oct. 1st		Office Routine	
	" 2nd		Marched from POUILLY to TUPIGNY (M.I. & Sheet 62B) and returned to POUILLY same day	
	" 3rd		Marched from POUILLY to TUPIGNY V.S. (M.I. & Sheet 62B) and returned to POUILLY same day	
POUILLY	" 4th		Remained at POUILLY	
	" 5th		Visited 'A' Canadian M.V.S., 14th M.V.S., HQ Canadian Cav Bde, HQ 7th Cavalry Bde & Royal Canadian Dragoons	
	" 6th		Visited 'A' Canadian, 13th & 14th M.V. Sections with D.D.V.S., Canadian Corps	
			Conference at Divisional HQ.	
	" 7th		Office Routine. 13th, 14th, & 'A' Can. M.V. Sections were demobilised in afternoon. 13th A.M.V.B. Sheet 62B great S.W. of BELLENGLISE. All three sections moved to G.30.B. Sheet 62B on morning 8th. 'A' Can M.V.S. remained at that spot and returned to POUILLY and rejoined their Brigade the same evening.	
	" 8th		Left POUILLY for operations 3 a.m. 13th & 14th M.V.S. again moved to G.28a Sheet 62B and thence to U.11.d.9.9. 13th M.V.S. subsequently moving forward afternoon to Operations U.21.B.6.2 Fermes. No 14 M.V.S. retaining the Collecting Vet Section & 13th M.V.S. the Vet Casualty Section. 'A' Can. M.V.S. ordered to move to GENEVE	
	" 9th		Operations. Returned to MONTIGNY. 14th M.V.S. moved from U.11.d.9.9. & P.9.a.4.0. Sheet 57B. NE of BERTRY.	
	" 10th		Remained at MONTIGNY. - Office Routine. 'A' Can. M.V.S. at GENEVE. 13th M.V.S. at FERMES and 14th M.V.S. at BERTRY.	
	" 11th		13th M.V.S. returned to GENEVE to assist A'Can M.V.S. as Collecting Post. Left at FERMES until 13th inst. 14th M.V.S. moved to O.18.B. Sheet 57B.	
	" 12th		Divisional Headquarters forwarded to BERTRY and thence to ELINCOURT same day.	
			Visited A' Canadian M.V.S. at GENEVE with A.A. & Q.M.G.	
	" 13th		Left ELINCOURT for BOIS de HENNOIS for D.D. & I. Visited A'Can. M.V.S. and 12 A.A. v.B. M.G. 13th & 14th M.V. Sections rejoined their Brigades	

Army Form C. 2118.

WAR DIARY
or
INTELLIGENCE SUMMARY.
(Erase heading not required.)

Page 2.

Place	Date	Hour	Summary of Events and Information	Remarks and references to Appendices
BOIS de HENNOIS	Oct. 14th	1st to 31st October (continued)	Visited H.Q. 7th Cavalry Brigade and 14th M.Y. Section	A Cdn. M.V.S. reported to Brigade afternoon. Stowed all
"	" 15th		Conference at Divisional H.Qrs. Office Routine	Transport Casualties
"	" 16th		Inspected animals of 7th M.G. Sqdn. Visited H.Q. Canadian Cavalry Bde. & A Cdn. M.V.S.	
"	" 17th		Conference of Veterinary Officers. Inspected animals of 3rd Field Squadron R.E. Visited 13th V.S. and 3rd Signal Squadron R.E.	
"	" 18th		Saw horses of 10th Royal Hussars, 3rd Dragoon Guards and squadron of 1st Royal Dragoons ed units. Inspected horses of 6th M.G. Sqdn and "C" Battery R.H.A.	
"	" 19th		Inspected animals of Light and Heavy Section, 3rd Cavalry Reserve Park. Office Routine	
"	" 20th			
"	" 21st		Inspected animals of Cdn. M.G. Sqdn and Local details. Horses visited Canadian Signal troop.	
"	" 22nd		Inspected animals of 1st Kings Horse	
"	" 23rd		" " " " 1st Royal Dragoons	
"	" 24th		Visited sick lines of 3rd Dragoon Guards. Saw horses of 3rd Dragoon Guards & 10th Royal Hussars at walk. Inspected 3rd Signal Squadron R.E. Visited 13th V.S.	
"	" 25th		Inspected animals of 3rd Cav. Div. A.S.T. Coy.	

Army Form C. 2118.

WAR DIARY
INTELLIGENCE SUMMARY.
(Erase heading not required.)

Instructions regarding War Diaries and Intelligence Summaries are contained in F. S. Regs., Part II. and the Staff Manual respectively. Title pages will be prepared in manuscript. Page 3

Place	Date	Hour	Summary of Events and Information	Remarks and references to Appendices
BOIS de HENNOIS	Oct. 26th		1st to 31st October (continued)	
"	" 27th		Office Routine	
"	" 28th		Office Routine	
"	" 29th		Inspected 13th M.V.S.	
"	" 30th		Inspected animals of Royal Canadian Dragoons and "A" Sec. M.V.S.	
"	" 31st		Inspected animals of K Battery R.H.A., 7th Dragoon Guards and 14th M.V.S.	
			Inspected horses of 16th Royal Hussars and 3rd Dragoon Guards	
			Inspected animals of D.A.C.	

O. Cantly
Lieut Colonel
A.D.V.S., 3rd Cavalry Division

Army Form C. 2118.

WAR DIARY
INTELLIGENCE SUMMARY.
(Erase heading not required.) A.D.V.S. 3rd Cavalry Division

981 36

Place	Date	Hour	Summary of Events and Information	Remarks and references to Appendices
BOIS de HENNOIS/Nov 1st	November 1st to 30th 1918			
	Nov 2nd		Office Routine	
	" 3rd		Inspected animals of Household Dragoons	
	" 4th		" " 17th Lancers	
	" 5th		Office Routine	
	" 6th		do - Very wet	
	" 7th		Marched from BOIS du HENNOIS to INCHY	
	" 8th		" " INCHY to DOUAI	
	" 9th		" " DOUAI to SAINGHIN	
	" 10th		Office Routine	
	" 11th		Marched from SAINGHIN to ANTOING	
	" 12th		ANTOING to TOURPES and returned to ANTOING. Armistice Day	
	" 13th		ANTOING Conference at Divisional HdQrs	
	" 13th		Visited 13th M.V. Section	
	" 14th		Conference at "Q" - Conference of Veterinary Officers of Division	
	" 15th		Office Routine	
	" 16th		Visited HQ 6th Cav Bde & 13th M.V.S.	

Army Form C. 2118.

WAR DIARY
INTELLIGENCE SUMMARY (continued)
(Erase heading not required.)

Instructions regarding War Diaries and Intelligence Summaries are contained in F. S. Regs., Part II. and the Staff Manual respectively. Title pages will be prepared in manuscript.

Place	Date	Hour	Summary of Events and Information	Remarks and references to Appendices
	Nov 1st to 31st/1918 (continued)			
	Nov 17th		Marched from ANTOING to BASSILLY	
	" 18th		" " BASSILLY to ENGHIEN	
ENGHIEN	" 19th		Office Routine	
	" 20th		Visit from Div. Cav. Corps. Visited 13th M.Y.S.	
	" 21st		Marched from ENGHIEN to WATERLOO	
	" 22nd		" " WATERLOO to PERWEZ	
PERWEZ	" 23rd		Visited H.Q. Canadian Cavalry Bde. & H.Q. 7th Cavalry Brigade.	
	" 24th		Marched from PERWEZ to MALÈVES - Ste MARIE WASTINES.	
MALÈVES - STE. MARIE - WASTINES	" 25th		Office Routine	
	" 26th		Visited 'A' Cdn. M.Y.S. & Fort Garry Horse. Visit from D.D.V.S. Cavalry Corps	
	" 27th		Visited Inniskilling Dragoons	
	" 28th		Office Routine	
	" 29th		Visited 'A' Cdn. M.Y.S. Lord Strathcona Horse	
	" 30th		Inspected animals of Lord Strathcona Horse & nucleus 'A' Cdn M.Y.S.	

O. Clark
Lieut Colonel
A.D.V.S., 3rd Cavalry Division

WAR DIARY or INTELLIGENCE SUMMARY

Army Form C. 2118.

H.Q.V.S. 3rd Cavalry Division

No. V8237

Place	Date	Hour	Summary of Events and Information	Remarks and references to Appendices
Field	1918 1st Dec.		DMO visits MALEVE STE MARIE NAISINES. Lt Col A.F. CLARKE A.D.V.S.	ADVS
	2		—	ADVS
	3		ADVS inspects horses Lord STRATHCONA HORSE	ADVS
	4		ADVS " Canadian Mtd Inf Station.	ADVS
	5		ADVS inspects horses 10th Royal Hussars.	ADVS
	6		" visits R Canadian Horse Artillery	ADVS
	7		" with D.E. Mt I to arrange evacuation of sick animals	ADVS
	8		Sergt HUGHES RAVC invalided sick.	ADVS
	9		ADVS visits 1st Royal DRAGOONS.	ADVS
	10			ADVS
	11		ADVS duty hours Lord STRACHONA Horse.	ADVS
	12		" attended inspection by G.O.C. of Canadian Cavalry Brigade.	ADVS
	13		ADVS visits Can mtd Inf Station in absence of Canadian STOMATIUS	ADVS
	14		—	ADVS
	15		Lt Col CLARKE ADVS admitted to C.C.S. NAMUR. Capt BURCS RAVC assumes duties ADVS	
	16		ADVS motors to SOHEIT TINLOT.	

Army Form C. 2118.

WAR DIARY
or
INTELLIGENCE SUMMARY.
(Erase heading not required.)

Instructions regarding War Diaries and Intelligence Summaries are contained in F. S. Regs., Part II. and the Staff Manual respectively. Title pages will be prepared in manuscript.

Place	Date	Hour	Summary of Events and Information	Remarks and references to Appendices
SHELT TRENCH	17/4/16		Inspection of Ammunition Column	
	18		"ASTS" inspect horse Am. Hors Transport & Reserve Park	
	19		hate 14 hrs. VIEN	
	20		ASTS Car Insp. with DADS with instructions for future work	
	21		DDS attends DATC on inspection of horse harness	
	22		do	6 Inf Bry
	23		do	7 Car. Bry
	24			
	25			
	26		ASTS visit horse Troops	
	27		Inspection of horses. 3 Can Crown Park.	
	28			Amethyst H6
	29		Cap. Burt. MILLS R.A.V.C. assumes duties ASSTs vice Capt BURT leg of for CANADA	
	30			
	31		ASTS visit 17 Lancers 7 SG.	

H Campbell Col
ADVS 3 Can
17/1/19

Army Form C. 2118.

WAR DIARY
or
INTELLIGENCE SUMMARY.

(Erase heading not required.)

A.D.V.S. 3rd Cavalry Division

9838

Place	Date	Hour	Summary of Events and Information	Remarks and references to Appendices
NANDRIN	1st		Office routine &c.	
	2nd		Visited 17th Lancers &c.	
	3rd	"	7th Dragoons &c &c	
	4th		Inspected 14th M.V.S. &c.	
	5th		Visited R.H.A. Amm Column inspected some suspected mange cases &c	
	6th		Office routine &c	
	7th		Inspected horses of Divisional &c.	
	8th		Went to LIEGE to ad statute to arrange for the disposal of urgent butcher cases &c	
	9th		Office routine &c	
	10th		Went to Canadian Base H.Q. to arrange for the classification of the horses in that Base &c	
	11th	"	Attended board at L.S.H. &c	
	12th	"	"	
	13	"	R.C.D.S. &c	

WAR DIARY
INTELLIGENCE SUMMARY

Army Form C. 2118.

ADYS. 3rd Cavalry Division

Place	Date	Hour	Summary of Events and Information	Remarks and references to Appendices
NANDRIN	1919. Jany 12		Lieut Col. H.G. REENFIELD RAVC reports for duty as Principal from 3rd Bri- and takes over duties ADVS 3rd Cav Div.	HQ.
"	13		Visit 5742 reserve general instruction. Spread & bandylights of horses. Classification hard working well from P.C.D. - good no aggregation on VOI. 20th Can Bde for working depicted on battached have but show hurugh.	H4
"	14		Inspection 17th Brand on marches. R Can Dragoons.	
"	15		Capt. O'BRIEN RAVC arrives and is detailed for duty with 2nd Dragoons HQ.	
			Lt. Burch inspects inspection Lines 3rd Cavry Horses horse forwards & good. and lines & billets good for.	
			Capt. THORNE RAVC arrives from No 2 Vety Hosp. & is detailed for duty with 1 Royal Dragoons. Lieut ELAM RAVC " 10 R Hussars	
"	16		Capt. F.G.HALBERT CAVC. VO7. FGH. proceeded on leave to UK. Vety Brand inspects horses, many F.G. Hosr. horses generally in good cond- and proc in the troops & cond. checked horses management of horses. Nearly all the horses shown & trained here.	HL
"	17		Vety Brand inspects horses. Can Can Bde HQ Can mud HQ Signals, 1 Can Can 2nd Bn. General condition of horses & good.	H4

WAR DIARY
or
INTELLIGENCE SUMMARY.
(Erase heading not required.)

Army Form C. 2118.

A.T.T.S. 3 Can Div

Place	Date	Hour	Summary of Events and Information	Remarks and references to Appendices
NANDRIN	July 18		Opening book of my Brand. outpost duties. Some Can MG Squad. inspected in 2 one store – cond. of mounts & grmt. well done. one. I have visited.	HQ
			Organiz. rapport of billets for tow theoriques etc. have arrived practical	
			no changes	
			hrs 4th Cdn extended to B.D.S. as follows: –	
			Rev. Artillery Total Cond. Horses bad Hors. Armory Total Strength	
		Hours	117 50 167 32 2 131 167 7923	
		noon	4 4 4 4 461 –	
	19		hd. Parenthys of horology Horses .057.	
			Leave for review at 6 Can Bde HQ Inder. —	
			en route there too busy & interesting for making up Brand diary from here	
	20		Hq Bond inspect horses – C Bat. R.t.A. Cond. v.good. Grounds – a Sc. 7 missing Rifle	HQ
			no Squad. 3 StG, horses cond. & good. Well cared for.	116
	21		" complete inspects 3 Se " " " "	117
			inspect 6CFA HQ. 13thMS SigCo. 6 Can F.A. D.D.V.S. inspect. approve natives	
	22			117
			drive along road behind & Sig Squad also inspect. A Squad. 10 Hussars. Horses	
			watch & obs. Land good. Count great home for land.	117

WAR DIARY
or
INTELLIGENCE SUMMARY.
(Erase heading not required.)

Army Form C. 2118.

Army: ASTA
3rd Cav Bde.

Place	Date	Hour	Summary of Events and Information	Remarks and references to Appendices
NANDRIN	16/1/21 Jan 23		Capt NICHOLAS RAMC reports to 2 Cav Bm. Capt O'CARROL 10.H. to 10 V.R.H.	
			Vet Board inspect horses H.Q. B Sqdn. 10 Hussars. Cond° Cans generally v. good.	H.g.
			Return to D.H.Q for arrangemt for Open Order.	
	"24		Inspect horses (V Board) H.Q. A Sqdn Royal Dragoons. Cond° Gen very good. 2 only worse time.	H.g.
	"25		6 M.G. Sqdn. Animals appear to be falling in condition	
			owing to hours of exercise. Forage & water poor. Shoeing & feet moderate. Individual	
			remark of finish in charge. Report silence in respect of horses having poor covers	
			V Board inspects (completion 6 CBde) 6 Sqdn Royal Dragoons. which has 70 per cent unmounted	H.g.
			horses f. bad volume. Shoes are generally not cared for	
			Return to DHQ	
	"26		Report arrangts for Cav Corps. Horse Collecting Camp. ENGIS. Lieut GLAPP RAMC. Attd.	
			Visit Qn report on overcrowding situation of horses. Suggest turning some horses out on duty &c.	
			sorry to cut shortage of men for grooming, which makes grooming time	
			necessity of thorough disinfection. Suggestion RSgnd R.Ds. 6 H.G.H 10 Hussars forthcoming.	
	"29		Weekly returns as follows submitted to DDVS Cav Corps.	
			Remain Admitted Sick Cured. Evacuated Sick Lost Remain. 2 oto2 Strength.	
			Horses 131. 152. 263 47. 161 2 2 71 263 7761.	
			Mule 4. Aog H 3 " 11 4 18 4436.	
			Total 2,547.	H.g.
			Mut horses	

Army Form C. 2118.

WAR DIARY
or
INTELLIGENCE SUMMARY.
(Erase heading not required.)

A/SJS. 3rd Cav Bn.

Instructions regarding War Diaries and Intelligence Summaries are contained in F. S. Regs., Part II. and the Staff Manual respectively. Title pages will be prepared in manuscript.

Place	Date	Hour	Summary of Events and Information	Remarks and references to Appendices
MANDRIN	1919 Jan 26		Submit weekly report to DDVS. Cond. of horses generally v. good, not excepting	HZ
"	" 27		Lecture previously. Then two o'clock with rec. of range (30 cases) against HZ. which proposals for checking other disease have been submitted.	HZ
"	" 28		Ref Brigade inspection K Battr RHA. Cond. + Care of horses v. good. Some skin-dis. bad. Horses count muddled.	HZ
"	"		C. Squad 6 doubt. dragons " " frequent v. good. 3 arms... grenades HZ	
"	"		HQ: A " 6 " " Cond. Care of horses v. good	
"	"		2 horses with clinical mange HQ. — v. Capt REIDY. Rare casualties to minstrations of ... irritation of ... HZ.	
"	"		B " 6 " " cond. Care + horses of horses protruding poor. HZ	
"	" 29		Horse shows v. Brigade inspects horses 2 Bd. HQ. 13 hrs. 7 C. 7 hrs. Horses + well done	HZ
"	"		7 S Cn SCHA. N. " Cond. + Care of horses v. good	
"	"		organizing ride for exhibition of class D horses. Board knows have all arranged for Candilled HZ	
"	" 30		Inspect horses 10 % SENY. HQ + C.Squad. Cond. horses generally v. good. 2 sore roof HZ.	
"	"		WARLEE + KERBAN Cond. Care + horses v. good. 2 cases of mange	HZ
"	"		Dispursed 7 Sh. KERBAN	
"	" 31		horses D + B Squadrons HQ. 17 Lancers. Cond. v. good. Many especially D + poor HZ	
"	"		Matter v wild. tanned. Horses making lots of travel v different throughout	
"	"		the week.	HZ

Army Form C. 2118.

WAR DIARY
or
INTELLIGENCE SUMMARY.
(Erase heading not required.)

Army: A.D.V.S. 3rd Cav. Divn.

Place	Date	Hour	Summary of Events and Information	Remarks and references to Appendices
	1919.			
NANDRIN	Jan 31.		Weekly Return as follows submitted to D.D.V.S. Cav. Corps.	
			Return: Admitted Total Cured Transferred Died Died Rem. Total Strength	
		Horses	71 178 249 26. 1 7 215 249 7649.	
		Mules	4 5 9 3 6 9 460.	
			Percentage of Wastage Horses 17.	
			" " Mules —	
			Weekly report to D.D.V.S. The Cmdt. of remounts 7 C. Bde. is to front - especially	
			B.S. Sq'd. 6 Smart Dragoons. Horses. 6. C. F. A. H.Q. 17 Lancers.	
			There are a large number of unsound horses C. Sq'nd 17 Lancers.	
			Mange figures continue to rise 43 cases admitted including 20 billeted sq'nd.	
			9. Hrsd Dragoons.	
			Suggestion has been put forward in organizating RAVC unit Can. Divn. that ADVS'k	
			have C.C. RAVC - he forms a special unit for special mange treatment inspection	
			& a return eight daily operations for mange. - Each unit to light horse amb. orders NCO.	
			had a stay kept in form of chart. all A whsm whelm 4 hours.	
			Submit weekly mange in curbis horses from Antwerp report that horses is assembled	

AS DS 3 Cav Dvy

A6915 Wt. W11422/M1160 350,000 12/16 D.D. & L. Forms/C/2118/14. on to ENGLAND.

WAR DIARY
or
INTELLIGENCE SUMMARY.
(Erase heading not required.)

Army Form C. 2118.

ADVS. 3 Cavly Divn

Vol 39

Place	Date	Hour	Summary of Events and Information	Remarks and references to Appendices
	1919			
MANDRIN	1 Feb		Weather V cold. Heavy snow impeded Vety Board but carried on. Inspected 7th L.G.R. & B.W.M. Condition & care of horses very good, a very nice old "C" Squadron. 17th Lancers Inspected. Good grounds & very large percentage of horses & tents horses.	
			A.V.A. bivs returned for horse losses as Divl Vety chain not included. VO1 did not understand. Cav Horses 2 & 3. Temporary chart revised & without my enquiry it.	
			Report rising of Mvd EVAM Camp – no material importance & immovable for a Enemy Boxes.	
			Captured Reports VO3 authorised to NSVS for France meeting & L.V.A.E. GARGE repr. late ADVS for two months.	H.Q.
	2 Feb		Telegraph to NSVS Cav Corps 180 horses assembly incineration at Div DPs for details of same & in centre of Zyp Guard Horses 7 Cav Bde = as no dispersed record of Regimental horses in the system.	
	3 Feb		Heavy snow. Vety Generals Inspected horses 3rd Bala Squadron 4th I.K.Dn in Heavy snow. DVS Consulted a principles A.V.A. Dvrs for Chem. Ho Div Chaise.	
			Opening October a trained for disinfection. Horse standing at Cav Corps Animal Colliery Compsr. after lack batch of horses horses passed through	H.Q

Army Form C. 2118.

WAR DIARY
or
INTELLIGENCE SUMMARY
(Erase heading not required.)

A.D.V.S. 3rd Cav Div.

Place	Date	Hour	Summary of Events and Information	Remarks and references to Appendices
	1919			
NANDRIN	3 Feb.		Stop inoculation CANADIAN D class horses when DOVS. + supply rly kind	
			on Belgian Govt. trucks all branch of The Rhine	
			Telegraph 5TVO divers mailers in order to convene Indian tcs. are heren	
			through Celebrity Camps.	
			CAPT DUFAULT CAVC proceeds in 4 days from to PARIS	Hr.
"	4 Feb.		Inspence of V.O.I at my office, on failure of empty unit now without mulas	
			up RTA DVO (to include) D class VH Camy) Capt. MIREDY CAVC does not	
			seem in authoriain of 2 divisi. cher on trosfr HO gha Bde.	
			Ht is arranged by G.O.C. 3rd Cav Bde at big instance	
			O. Thind Caparna BSFQ on Expert. Cavalry BU. G. 107 8. also G.O.G. instruction	
			Vet Board inspects hence 3rd Field Squadron + 5TFQ. mule btty. Cdn HQ	
			huni front RAFC to car arf. Collin carp service in depth.	
	5 Feb.		Heavy fall of snow in night.	16t.
			Vet Board inspects horses RHA. and Signal Sqn., MSC Hq. horses	
			well done + excellent condition especially RHA. hors Am DVC due in tomorrow	16t.
			Practice of Blind Horse, Opthalmia Cases	
	6 Feb.		Vet Board inspect mules Reserve Park + A.H.T.C. MIDAVE. Cond. v good.	16t.

Army Form C. 2118.

WAR DIARY
or
INTELLIGENCE SUMMARY.
(Erase heading not required.)

A.S.V.S. 3rd Cavalry Bde.

Place	Date	Hour	Summary of Events and Information	Remarks and references to Appendices
NAMDR.N.	1919. July 6th		Report. Case sent to ENGLAND - Capt HALBERT C.A.V.C.	
			Sick horse: 22. Isolated for observation of all case not regular in Bde, to DDVS.	
			Vety Board. Inspected horses RCHA. HQ 2MG. Cond: good, a large proportion	
			"A Bn RHA. Cond: care general & good. " of lean horses	
			Vety returns submitted to DDVS. Cav Corps as follows.	
			Remain Admitted Died Cured Evacuated Bde Destroyed Cannis. Dols Shingles	
	Horses	315 142 2 357 27 2 287 357 74 55		
	Mules	6 6 - 12 4 - 1 7 12 45		
			Percentage of wantage Horses '37%.	
			mules '27%.	
			Weekly Report. Cond. of animals, Dust Storms is generally & good, especially 15th Q	
			Mtd R.H.A. : Bde Am Col. Rise in figures of manage is continued	
			This is on a large measure due to more strenuous supervision.	
			Clipping & other precautions known previously barraith	
	8th		Vety Board inspected horses B Coy RCHA -	
			Brit Core been transferred in 3rd Car Bde. Pte WINGATE 14 Hus A.V.C.	

WAR DIARY
or
INTELLIGENCE SUMMARY.   Adv. S. 3rd Cav Bde.

Army Form C. 2118.

(Erase heading not required.)

Place	Date	Hour	Summary of Events and Information	Remarks and references to Appendices
	1919		arranged	
MAYDRIN	Feb 9	1930	Sick animals forwarded to AD Vet Hosp CHARLEROI from ENGRS attached	
			One wounded mule - no orders received overnight - no unclassified received	
			to D. class for D.D. exp. to La. vent.	46
	" 10		Found there is no stock exylin on hand - 9 wounds arranged a	
			batch in hosp. Some were sent home in batches not too temporary	
			well - hacken got onto us on numbers of horses - 20 animals arrived to horses	
			+ sour week scrub instructions as MTS. began + without notifications	
			Capt. O'BRIEN posted to Cav Corps + here collecting camp. JESSAINS	
			re action outside to him as regards of wellness info orgns posted thin	
			Standi + Return SOTS details of horses who have been class 2 for sale	
			in DVs capture to dispatch fragment of Lance arm available but subreg	
			disposal information of 220 dup. cases as batt (inspection) (any) however	
			instructions DVS. instructions to Board. It being intended to ship ack'g	
			this close but then to Corps. This is however cancelled later	
	" 11		Inspected 6 MG Squad from which some 30 cases of mange have reported	MS
			Any advise report on visit to DDVO - Condition here improved - generally	

Army Form C. 2118

WAR DIARY
or
INTELLIGENCE SUMMARY.
(Erase heading not required.)

Place	Date	Hour	Summary of Events and Information	Remarks and references to Appendices
NANDRIN	11 July 1918		Generally quiet. Clipping of the mens' interior enabled a patch road test complete. Completion available and capitation not acceptable — accommodation at palace [supposed?] to be all accounted which I suggest to the army bill took to the army place. Men's morning inspection tended to stick men out of hoe. Visit IAD a Sqdn 1st Royal Dragoons reference to emergency outbreak, suggest Clipping on short now allotting of women as a prophis spread — proposed by Low-long head out. But super of trays - isolated suggest have turned out & roll & am looks — troops helped - absent to be employed as hoe. To improve, to steal overapped thought have by Emma troops. Visit Gainsby, that material at 13 rounds decade of the Colgin horses. Were he Inspect Engis — Car bogs there Clicking [Campa?] magnesity & car of home when are introduction for home on out known barrage of suspense arid when it had to moving a delay to change [Regn?] to 1510 D, 6550 T, soft in condition for horses for horses - for handles underground sleeps out important protection than before. In with two here, then on a building probably [protected rate?] of rest thunderstorm fell — shown probable hour, 5 ft high iron beds and	

WAR DIARY
or
INTELLIGENCE SUMMARY.

Army Form C. 2118.

AAVS, 3rd Cavalry Corps

Place	Date	Hour	Summary of Events and Information	Remarks and references to Appendices
NANDRIN	1919 Sep 11		SECRET EVENTS.— Visit Car Corps to know camp just commenced (10th inst) organization & care of horses regard. With any part commenced. Selvins the records for a negative time is other than those known are not adverted to others. Was received by S.O. & requested all remaining D show horses notify 15 DAYS the horses sale to Britishers, but appeared in addition be put in LEGG on any train recommenced to AD V^{ef} AP	
"	"		I inspired all Hy^g Guard horses 7th C^o Bde arr in good thoroughbred. Will a difficulty to keep breeding of colt line contact with English Thoroughbreds I for ones for improved Champions to be found by around ~ Sri an (4 months, advanced to DD.V.S but by others which will be free (4 months. ~ Sire cobs in syls) & Stins 6 month horses normal for which J suggest cobs.	16L
			This all cancelled DVS decides horse to go to ENGLAND but & month from last time is rgt (imputation of data normal) n 16 can be cast as men here.	

Indry AAVDS K Both report no front ayt anointed Ty's J other being received are drawn from men ant any take legged 16L

WAR DIARY
or
INTELLIGENCE SUMMARY.
(Erase heading not required.)

Army Form C. 2118.

ADVS 3rd Cav Bde

Place	Date	Hour	Summary of Events and Information	Remarks and references to Appendices
NANDRIN	1919 Feb 13		Insp 3rd Cav Corps cards for details X.4.2. of all horses here. Chief - Anthrax. Many RDVs & 2 horses for destruction. VO LSH made no report to inspection known of this regt + F Gun Horses has been stopped till it is complete. Q office instituted & records figures for horse cards of horses rejected by DDVS class admission of returns of horses for RVS, no VOs back records from RVs &c Lately Return as follow Animals 5 DDVS Con Corps Remain Admitted 3rd C Cav Invaliped Died Estroyed Rem Total Strength 289 188 425 44 171 2 153 425 7451 Horse 8 8 8 3 8 416 Mule 4 1 Percentage of wastage (Horse '37) (Mule '22) Report to DDVS. Cond. of horses generally good - no change since decrease percent of horses and since I took my duties. Not my inspection of horses made suggests outbreak in hand when shown Eve occurred last	79¾

Army Form C. 2118.

WAR DIARY
or
INTELLIGENCE SUMMARY.

Army 3rd Can. Div.

(Erase heading not required.)

Instructions regarding War Diaries and Intelligence Summaries are contained in F. S. Regs., Part II. and the Staff Manual respectively. Title pages will be prepared in manuscript.

Place	Date	Hour	Summary of Events and Information	Remarks and references to Appendices
KANDRIN	16/9 Feb 14		Written to D.H.Q. asking for [illegible] through by local authority asking for employment for civilian authorities	
	"15		G.O.C. [illegible] approved of D. Haven & Battery by H/q opinion has been a date to [illegible] there here. He approves of suggestion to procure them [illegible] workers to procure [illegible] as [illegible] opinion who will certify that [illegible] as to [illegible] cannot attend sales everywhere [illegible] was. From [illegible] of 7 or 8 hours for sale is not the warranted to [illegible] railway to our nearest [illegible] unless [illegible] a Wholly to [illegible] [illegible] value of [illegible] [illegible]. G.O.C. approves of [illegible] of horses [illegible] at [illegible] which is urgently required before the [illegible] starts.	
	"16"		D/S [illegible] in reply to my application. Canadian [illegible] will decide disposal of those known CANADIAN under a [illegible] at Can. [illegible] to [illegible] figures to G.O.C. [illegible] horse class D which is [illegible] to [illegible] or [illegible] pain trunk suggests than disposed - Meanwhile to return for decision at [illegible] of BELGIAN Govt.	

WAR DIARY
or
INTELLIGENCE SUMMARY.

Army Form C. 2118.

(Erase heading not required.)

Army... 3rd Cav Div.

Instructions regarding War Diaries and Intelligence Summaries are contained in F. S. Regs., Part II. and the Staff Manual respectively. Title pages will be prepared in manuscript.

Place	Date	Hour	Summary of Events and Information	Remarks and references to Appendices
MAY DR IV	1919 Feb 15		Weather Change. Heavy mist, apt 3 inch snow frost. Visit Cav Camps & Horse Camps. Arrange with Works for disinfection for Forsicht. Submit DDVS it will be impossible for our V.O. to do whole work for 10,000 horses than I stock inspection & work for 100 firs & our vet dept as will as other camps in no other V.O. available. I did 2 x 3 x 2 from this issue for the purpose.	15
			Wire DDVS by Telegram & Instruction having received & send horse C. Return to England. Horses to ENGLAND. Horses to be Entrained with easier than are bigger for purpose. Neither Bret for SWS complete over Fox Gatery Horse practically all D. Horse.	15
"	Feb 16		Got to Boulogne.	
			Reconnaissance. DDVS what horse than C cannot be sent to ENGLAND. Visit 14 Brig. Inspect vet remounts. General arrangements for NCOs men & horses Hq.	Hq
"	17		Attend Conference DHQ re dispatch of Class C horse to ENGLAND. Report all Cav Wheelers Wheelers. Necrotic Brouchitis cases Chromicitis for horse figures good now each horse (by multi squadron) affected with Bletcherma or OPN. bricus and liberal consent B — notify that to ship Forward horses con horse hopes 23rd March 1919 (Orders DVS 15/9/19) and Ind nf.	
"	18		Arrangement now complete to come works of Horse intend (order have coming in ENGLAND) DVS. at 1st Cav Corps Horse Camps for that I have not enough V.O. to work on account of heavy intake in the remainder of all	

16.

Army Form C. 2118.

WAR DIARY
or
INTELLIGENCE SUMMARY.
(Erase heading not required.)

Instructions regarding War Diaries and Intelligence Summaries are contained in F. S. Regs., Part II. and the Staff Manual respectively. Title pages will be prepared in manuscript.

Place	Date	Hour	Summary of Events and Information	Remarks and references to Appendices
	1919			
NANDRIN	Feb 18		Driving to & out 3 Fair trade C horse C ENGLAND then wrote & sent proce—	
			LIEGE 100 i day	
			DD'S visits Cav Corps. 3 hour camp + i m pleased with the arrangements.	
			It appears satisfactory. from being unwanted at ENG's and expresses disgusted	
			He appears anxious of dropped troops carr'd although very slight as I	
			saw many all sick as far as possible being signed brothing of animals	
			from horses.	
			I am unable to fill vacancies have a sudden archive returned to Cranston horses	
			R.D.Y's inspec'n Cav Corps Cavalry Corps ENG'S, approves of m'y report that	
			he is unsuited for horses.	
			I visit & have long talks with for the two V.O's there	
			Arrive FERGUSSON CAT proceeds on leave to ENGLAND.	
			Lt Col Cav Od approves my organisation disposition of VO's & organisation of	
	19.		VO's who work round to new centres thus this Area (not an humitifive) it is	A2.
			impossible. will present claim I wrote for it to L. S. Thorne.	
			hen O.V. GUNNING CAT. reports for duty with 2nd GARDE HOUSE.	A2.

WAR DIARY
of
INTELLIGENCE SUMMARY.
(Erase heading not required.)

Army Form C. 2118.

AVS 3rd Cavly Div

Place	Date	Hour	Summary of Events and Information	Remarks and references to Appendices
MANDRIN	1918 Feb 19		Arrange the STKD. all Lys Evac. horses to be changed C.B. for cold in the country, and special changes retained by each Est. when to reinforce out.	147
			Class DS 15/2/19.	
	20		Inspected by Asst Dir Vety Serv Army Troops & AVS Brit 1st Cav Div on motorised STKD.	
			I inspected & changed w/ref Brit 1 Oxford mounted shepherd which is	
			approved by G.C. 3rd Can Div, form of exact work as follows.	
			SERANG Sani Carps. Green Tnps. 109A. 110 #114 Rly Bns. 147 A.T.C. R.E.	
			ENG3 193 Labr C. FRONE R.C. C. R.E. Guard Hosps.	
			Animals generally in good condition. Sell cared for.	147
			Another bad ulcer has been seen.	
	21		Visit STKD. Report on inspection labour unit G.O.C. entrust the necessity for	
			keeping disinfection of anything the for return to England.	
			Wrote to Empress OC. AVS to Egypt of Cambt Hy Sect re sanitation kit	
	22		when G.C. 3rd Can Div.	
			wire.	147
			Submit report & recom & DDVS re follows. hys horses C class ENGLAND - duty cobs w/ Regts	
			in unit entailed hug of horse	

WAR DIARY or INTELLIGENCE SUMMARY

Army Form C. 2118.

A.V.S. 2nd Corps

(Erase heading not required.)

Instructions regarding War Diaries and Intelligence Summaries are contained in F.S. Regs., Part II. and the Staff Manual respectively. Title pages will be prepared in manuscript.

Place	Date	Hour	Summary of Events and Information	Remarks and references to Appendices
NANDRIN	1919 July 23		With the necessary concentration of horses at 2 Corps Horse Camps — N & S	SECAKS ENGS
			There VO's now employed on this camp activity.	
			Generally horses are arriving there in good condition. Vy. work is being completed on to feeding. Stabling & etc. compared to an ideal normal in 3 or so hours	
			Tend of present Animal strength:— Horses pair Mules 6 beginning	
			Runs — Admrtd. Std. Lomd. Unfrent std. Enfrent Pres. Total Strength	
			153 97 250 41½ 70 2 18t 1 118 3 250	
			3 476	
			× 14 D. Coun.	
		Horses	Proceeding & training. shoes 1.07.	
		Mules	mules .237.	
"	July 24		Art. chut & V.D. statistics tpr. Brand for Chart week ends before consolidated for agros-CDS. H.Q.	H.Q.
"	" 24		Visit Y & CP. and check elongation of horses regards & sick with VO.	H.Q.
			Interview Lieut GUNNING GAVC & gave him instructions for his month in Command	
"	" 25		Visit Std Cav. Cw Regt. & offer scheme approved organize traitement &	
			disposal of sick animals by this Regt. when it lemme bart area shortly.	
			Visit horse order at LIEGE	H.Q.

WAR DIARY
or
INTELLIGENCE SUMMARY.

Army Form C. 2118/19

ADVS 2nd Cavalry.

Place	Date	Hour	Summary of Events and Information	Remarks and references to Appendices
MANDRIN	1919 July 26		Arrange check throughout tomorrow of all Chevrograins of all animals in division of all sick reported in Cav. Corps	
			Visit DDVS Cavalry Corps SPA	Aps
	" 27		Inspect & Chevogd transport arrived at ENGIS. Cav Corps Animal Camp	
			Visit B Squadron 10 Hussars arrangs Chevograd over D/S animals	
			Instrust O.C. 13 troops in respect of no returns rendered. Any escape from	
			Visit Cav lines 3 Hussars Camps SERANG. Pointing to Commanding Officer of Horses unsuitable for sale —	
			asked leave recommended. Arrange Chevograd & pattern to be Fitted upon order — remainder of	
			to a Butchery Chev D	
			& put up for auction not sentable unanimous forces. Proceed to LIEGE	
			various Sub Areas & arrange visits here for three chapeaud	
			Order VO RCD & return from D/S at this Camps to be right about to have Ammn	
			arrange for V.O. ENG/S to keep these ans on available to instruct SERANG	
			camps 1000 horses — constantly hg" turned over for sale.	Aps
	" 28		Visit 6 Scenic Sgns inspect supervise sup ing Chevograd & sick Ret rgl. K Bat't RHA	
			7 M.g Sqdn & check into Chevograd & records.	

H Campbell Col
ADVS 2nd Cav of 15mm

Army Form C. 2118.

WAR DIARY
or
INTELLIGENCE SUMMARY.
(Erase heading not required)

ADVS. 3rd Cavalry Division

Place	Date	Hour	Summary of Events and Information	Remarks and references to Appendices
MANDRIN	1919. March 1		Visit DSVO. report to O. Veterinary arrangements for Imperial Service officers for return march to Germany.	
			See office Home Orders for future march of Division.	
			Re Visit: made final arrangements with Cav. Cav. Bde. H.Q. + Can. Vet. Sec.	
			Surprise visits at ADVS office to be relieved from Can. Cav. Bde. at present.	
			Inspected Reports & officers returned to DDVS after depositing higher authorities for transmission to Lt. Col. CLARKE FAVC for his records.	AC.
"	2.		Divisional papers - reports Can. Cav. Bde. forwarded to ADVS. Canadian Corps.	
			Opening amendments and delivery of Divisional Control to Belgium head vet authorities.	
			Approved by Brevet Agreement (Veterinary Branch)	15a.
"	3		Inspection amends and clarify amends [?] forward met seen by Vet Brand of A.H.T.Co. MODAVE and 3rd Cav. Rec. Park. TERWAGNE. Very well. Army & respect:	14.
"	4		Dull wet day. Visit Q. French Claims for Brevet, Cav thence 271. All V. by.	
			Arrange for dispatch N.G.os from on stretch bearer allotment for MARCH.	17.
"	5.		Submit to DDVS details of non returnable lots forwarded by HQs open BASE. Gradual letting orders to man ACs open 7 mon.	
			Changing to notice to an otherwise on 14 days leave to ENGLAND.	
			Capt. M. V. HILL RAVC proceeds on 14 days leave to ENGLAND.	14.

WAR DIARY
or
INTELLIGENCE SUMMARY.
(Erase heading not required.)

Army Form C. 2118.

A.D.V.S. 3rd Cavalry Div.

Place	Date	Hour	Summary of Events and Information	Remarks and references to Appendices
NANDRIN	1919 Jan 6.		Very hot. Visit D.D.V.S. Cav. Corps at SPA for instructions - arrived ecenile during rapid forages of orgs for D.T.C. half ton lorries M.T. party stooly E. B.M.E. It is hoped to turn to newly hiroples heat 01640 for M.T. troples enjoined. Little procedure from hospital to much work, to other to write. Submit report in total M.T. board Chargeable of stores - rather + rather if all animals in Diria.	Htz.
"	" 7.		Visit O.M.S.sives only rapid dimot by drain of Drain - c 1300 horses away from 1st Cav Divn.	Htz.
"	" 8.		Dropped sick avails recount. 14 HH at VIEW - arrange for sick uncle . Ord. C. Britten Submit to D.D.V.S. Cav. Corps weekly returns + report as follows :- to trait at N.S. H.Q.	Htz.
			Running Admitted Total 6 and Transferred Sick Sick losts. Employment Remaining Total Strength of this week	
		Horses	136 38 174 30 4 75 65 174 2459	
		Mules	9 12 21 4 17 21 6.8	
			Percentage of horses sick those 167. mules Nil.	Htz.

Army Form C. 2118.

WAR DIARY
or
INTELLIGENCE SUMMARY.   Asst. 3rd Cavalry Division
(Erase heading not required.)

Place	Date	Hour	Summary of Events and Information	Remarks and references to Appendices
	1919			
MANDRIN	Mar 7		Report = Condition : strength of arms : no change = generally very good. Note of men 2nd 3rd Cav Bdes from diary temp, most complete. Transport working well. Divnl rendezvous of heavy regimes = c Bde RHA not well & reported = full	N.B.
			horses taken as necessary.	N.B.
	8		Inspect horn RR cattle sect. type much to RHINE report Q. they are capable of proving (only ing. to unit opinion) but horses should be light as horses reduced.	
			Inspect all arab. annuals. 13 hrs. STOCKAY. arrange for date return 7 approx annual reports for expenses of hospital tractor. arrange inoculation 7 Marandbi. Start of 14 hrs. on Thursday 10th inst.	
			thought annual report & make necessary alteration & exploration. date not to report O.C. & expenses only arranged & R.A. concentration at CHOKIER 10th inst.	
			Visit Ca Corps Annual Camps ENGIS . SERANG . both much improved v. unf. good HQ att.	
	9		Conference D.H.Q. on relation to cairo 3 rafts. deep and other units. dispatch HQs to 1st Cav Bw dispersal of all 3 horses. 1st Cav Bw transport to take for all. tomm 4/4/19	N.B.

WAR DIARY
or
INTELLIGENCE SUMMARY.

Army Form C. 2118.
23.

A.V.S. 3rd Cav Bde

(Erase heading not required.)

Place	Date	Hour	Summary of Events and Information	Remarks and references to Appendices
NANDRIN	1919 Nov 9.		Scheme approved by G.O.C. that horses to concentrate in open during three rapid marches on MEUSE and fully inspected with range of t to 7 mm of lor transport though it. Men work over to concentrate horses each unit of impetd places especially CLERMONT & AMAY. Organise special parties, action of all injected buildings. Organise V.O. command for this measure - which is all cancelled at night.	
			Report to D.D.V.S. to French horse trade by 3rd Cav Bde 1919.	A2.
"	" 10.		Visit incorination RA horses proceeding with them from troop work of Bde to 3rd Cav Bde died with sick nearish. (CHORIER)	
"	"		Visit 9 horse camp - leps hork 44 sick much arrange for severals sick by special truck train to A.D. vet HP CHARLEROI. 25 horses - males every ask for history so others ask of which have not been effected. which are unsuitable to commerce treatment at vet Hospital.	A2.
"	" 10		Notify DTP authority for evacuation & order 13. 14 mls. (DYS 3497 9. C.19) and vet unit hors NCO horse attendants who are to proceed & army 9 occupation	A2.

Army Form C. 2118.
24.

WAR DIARY
or
INTELLIGENCE SUMMARY.

(Erase heading not required.)

A.D.V.S. 3rd Cavalry Div

Instructions regarding War Diaries and Intelligence Summaries are contained in F. S. Regs., Part II. and the Staff Manual respectively. Title pages will be prepared in manuscript.

Place	Date	Hour	Summary of Events and Information	Remarks and references to Appendices
	1919.			
MANDRA	Mar 11		Orders received for 4 regts to proceed 1st Cav Div & first concentration area here and 3 regts of 2nd Cav Div to come here for return to cadre. Also for 13th Horse moving here for ord'e troops to ENGLAND & FRANCE for both.	
			Signaling HQ works — V.O.s to proceed with regts in question notify DHQ. DDVS — ADVS 1st Cav Bri.	
			Visit DHQ repts situation at 3 horse camps etc — other full plans for remounts. Transmissions out of 13th 1st Cav Div — Cav base horse repd tel 27 transfr(?).	
			Arrang it not before 2nd Cav Bri V.O. here at my request for this afternoon duty but cannot recommendation for him when to visit on Capt O'BRIEN's (w/o 3 Cav)	
			Ambulance arrived immediately by DKS.	
			Submit from Cav horse 271 Brown Army of Occupation all NCOs men RMC 3rd Cav Div on been proposed candidates to for men on return ???, which has obtained hosh hertofore.	
			Arrange for transportation & moves of 13.3.14 mjs. during period till then. Moves to Cabir — Notify V.O.s of ??? of each, the orders march. Arrange for remounts ??? reports ?? moves ????	Hs. Hs. Hs.
			from dates instructions to 13.3.14 trust on Egypt outwance & rly & common for interchange.	

Army Form C. 2118

25

WAR DIARY
or
INTELLIGENCE SUMMARY.
(Erase heading not required.)

A.D.V.S. 3rd Cavalry Division

Instructions regarding War Diaries and Intelligence Summaries are contained in F. S. Regs., Part II. and the Staff Manual respectively. Title pages will be prepared in manuscript.

Place	Date	Hour	Summary of Events and Information	Remarks and references to Appendices
MANDRIN	1919 Mar 12		Capt. P. O'BRIEN R.A.V.C. (whose immediate demobilization to arranged for) on orders D.D.S received 11th inst) attached to 50 C.C.S. with fractured clavicle from 8/Horse Camp Jim relay arranged. Lieut ELAM R.A.V.C. v.o. Cav Corps & Horse Camps admitted to 50 C.C.S. with GASTRITIS. arranged V.O. 1 Royal Dragoons pated for duty	
"	"		Visit Horse Camp ENGIS. inspect arrivals ending 3 & 13 inst. > harge 1 Spotten	
"	" 13		Visit R.T.O with proposal for evacuation of sick as D.D.P.S. instruct CHARLEROI hospital closed. bring with D.A.D.O.S. for transport & mrs arrived Egypt. Inspect 1000 horse arrived today SERANG Camp from 1st Cav Div. now	V.G.
"			west return to hurt V.O. of the Camp for both	
"	" 14		Report to Q. & O/c R.A.V.C reinforcements continued absence at HOLROYD R.A.V.C. has tapsed ENGLAND to order that it may be completed hype when return to Cobham 36/4/19 D.V.S arms published to visit & report arrivements Mf5 Egypt O.C. R.A.V.C.	
"			Notify D.D.R. Sinh Open. O.C. Cav Corps Camp. ENGIS. Mrs hospital for mrs of Mf5 hospital of R.P. S.S. hurro later fuel particulars Under O.K. special debring from hospital of R.P. S.S. hurro later fuel particulars return on argument 0.16.40 at how warranted out from ENGIS Camp.. 10th R HUSSARS hem Div (V.O. Lieut ASTON from 1st Cav Dv.) & march 1st Cav Dr Hd	

A6945 Wt. W14922/M1160 350,000 12/16 D.D. & L. Forms/C/2118/14.

26.

Army Form C. 2118.

WAR DIARY
or
INTELLIGENCE SUMMARY.
(Erase heading not required.)

Advs. 3rd Cavalry Division

Place	Date	Hour	Summary of Events and Information	Remarks and references to Appendices
NANDRIN	1919 Jan 15		Visit office DDVS Cavalry Corps. reference to the remounts and sick arranged for issue of sick in unit lines also Meloxine (?) being arranged for. Cathy. Instructions re disposal of flour – also re for instruction of 2 MVS being issued to corps – report VOs connected to one C.I. Car Div. remounts as to the for work there. Arrangements for stores transports to proceed to 2 Horse camps for him my few weekly returns & reports controlled to DDVS Cav Corps as follows:	Hq.
			Remounts Admitted Total Issued Destroyed Sick total Remounts total Strength	
		Strong	65 111 176 44 69 2 35 26 176 1750	
			17 16 33 2 10 11 10 33 667	
			Percentage of wasting Horses '67'. Mules '31'.	
	16		Troops & stretchers for British figures high from 1st & 2nd Cav Div Horses all two brn Corps Horse concentration camps.	Hq.
	17		Visit 13 MVS unit detail instructions for demobilization EM&VS Camps is important. On road to SERANG camp is occupied for ex'd Bucks. I Q horses.	Hq.

WAR DIARY or INTELLIGENCE SUMMARY.

A.D.V.S. 3rd Cavalry Div

Army Form C.2118
27

Place	Date	Hour	Summary of Events and Information	Remarks and references to Appendices
MANDRIN	1919 Nov 18		Submit to D.D.V.S. Cav Corps total figures available from both 1 British Cav & remounts. They are incomplete as can get no reply for Canadian Bde. Left the town now to ENGLAND. Intn'd Canadian's account he arranged check on his figures in the form & will show more horses — or which should they have sold? 6 Senator Bragam. V.O. Capt REIDY Pape leave today for polite tour. 1 Regt arrange. V.O. Capt THORNE Pavé. 2nd injurer detta. O.C. Pet Rmnts Do knl. ordrs per V.O. Capt REIDY who has failed to comply with orders reported. 3 or 4 times arrival of Horses apply to SDVS Cav Corps for V.O. 17 horses. En route to Germany — as horses available here. He is briefed to provide me.	Hz
"	" 19		13 mls home to AMAY. From Hqt Horses hired whom they order. I inspect arrivals 3rd Remr Park RAMELOT. Conditions come good. Visit 3rd Rm Park at TERWAGNE & inspect ordt. Rode 17 horses to V.O. available from them horsd. & arrange for that out. Visit 4 horses 11 horses 3rd Suy Guard. arrived from 11 S.C. Sec. for exchange as Cadres. Visit 13 mls with instruction for ont. & O.C. Hy attendance undrve at CITOKIER. OMARET. RAUSA & AMAY	Hz

Army Form C. 2118
28

WAR DIARY
or
INTELLIGENCE SUMMARY.
(Erase heading not required.)

ADvS. 3rd Cavalry Div.

Place	Date	Hour	Summary of Events and Information	Remarks and references to Appendices
MANDRIN	1914 Nov 19		Visit RHA HQ at CHOISIER. Inspected sick & lame at SERANG Camp & returned 9 for evacuation. Journey to (4th Army) to obtain intg equipt. to complete units named to the return to Centre. 9, 10th March, horseback rs Adv Hd-Qtrs - CHARLEROI. Closed.	A/2
"	20		Hard & cold. Heavy snow squalls. Ground steep, damp return. All into equipt with units diminishing or being returned to Centre to be handed in to nearest M.V.S. a circ. speech submitted to D.H.Q. by O.C. units that this is completed with	A/2
"	21		Orders recd from D.V.S. that I was to remove sick ADvS 1st Cav Div. Report to D and arrange preliminary handing over to Capt. J Mills, RAVC.	
"	22		Weekly returns submitted to DDvS. 3rd Cav Div. Bringing group & unit. Remin. total Strngth	

		Remain	Admitted	Total	Cured	Dead	return	Remain	total Strength
Horses		26	77	103	20		25*	46	103 1449
Mules		10	4	14	8		2	4 + 14	659

Percentage of Wastage Horses 1.58
Mules .3.

* 14 Cav Corps Camps

A/2h

2353 Wt. W3544/1454 700,000 5/15 D.D.& L. A.D.S.S./Forms/C. 2118.

Army Form C. 2118.

WAR DIARY
or
INTELLIGENCE SUMMARY.
(Erase heading not required.)

A.D.V.S. 3rd Cavalry Division

Place	Date	Hour	Summary of Events and Information	Remarks and references to Appendices
NANDRIN	1919 Mar 25		D.H.Q — Visit Q. arrange for horse box in by transport to 1st Cav Divn	
"	26th		Inspect sick animals 3 horse camps. SERANG arrange for dust coloss to finish an inoculation for epi or Intlums. Heavy snow on ground	
"	27th		Stand by duties. to Capt J.H. Dixus RAVC - proceed to 1st Cav Divn	
	28th		H.Q. recd details of inspection of vet. equipmt. + all indents for Horsepital Kits, requirements.	
	29th		Visit H.Q. Animal collecting camp. Enlist 2 horse depot SERAING. Asst Sadler	
	30th		Routine work. Gas arranged with L. Officer to move to AMAY. Moved from NANDRIN to AMAY. arranged with L. Officer to send sick horses by road to DUREN	
	31st		Submitted the weekly returns to D.D.V.S. Car Corps. arranged for sick horses 2nd Car Divn to join truck horses from 5th Car Divn. Detailed Capt C.J.C. Ryan RAVC to proceed with batch of horses leaving for 1st Car Divn reporting himself on arrival to A.D.V.S. 1st Car Divn. Routine work	

J.M. [signature]
F. Capt. R.A.V.C.
A.D.V.S. 3rd Cav Divn

WAR DIARY

Army Form C. 2118.

A.D.V.S.

INTELLIGENCE SUMMARY. 3rd Cav. Div.

for April 1919

Vol 41

Instructions regarding War Diaries and Intelligence Summaries are contained in F. S. Regs., Part II. and the Staff Manual respectively. Title pages will be prepared in manuscript.

Place	Date	Hour	Summary of Events and Information	Remarks and references to Appendices
AMAY	1st		2 Lame dispd SERAINGE closed down. 4908 horses passed through the dipot. Sick by Authm 2828 fd to butchr 129 Ist to armd colly Coy. 1845 2 13 M.V.S. 257 3rd Car Jevin Pk SO. Animal received 1st Car Div 1759 2nd Car Div 1458 3rd Car Div 1502 Car. Depot 181 13 M.V.S. 3 Animal collecting Coy 2nd & 7th 2 arvd 1	
	2nd		Inspected Horse collecting camp Engis Routine work	
	3rd		Inspected R.P. & S.S. horses being sent to base from animal collecting Camp ENGIS. 288 horses dispatched	
	4th		Had one horse destroyed of 14 & 4 M.V.S. fracture pastern off later return for M.O. Sch.	
	5th		Sick leighly return to D.P.V.S. 4 th are a suspected Horse collecting camp ENGIS	
	6th		Routine work	
	7th		Inspected 368 horses dispatch to base from Horse collecting Camp ENGIS	

(2)

WAR DIARY of D.A.D.V.S.
INTELLIGENCE SUMMARY. 3rd Cav Div
(Erase heading not required.)

Army Form C. 2118.

Place	Date	Hour	Summary of Events and Information	Remarks and references to Appendices
AMAY	8th		Arranged for the dispatch of 7 relieved men surplus to Cadre to be sent to No 4 Vety. Hospital Calais	
"	9th		7 men dispatched to No 4 Vety. Hosp. Calais. Visited & annual collecting Camp E.N.G.I.S. Inspected all the animals there	
"	10th		Office Routine	
"	11th		Made out weekly returns for D.R.V.S. Received information that Capt Myhill R.A.V.C. would not return to 3rd Cav Div, but would remain in England to await demobilization	
"	12th		Routine visit visited Camp at E.N.G.I.S	
"	13th		Office Routine	
"	14th		Visited Annual collecting Camp E.N.G.I.S	
"	15th		Office Routine	
"	16th		Wired to DDVS about demob. also Dept Lucas also about Capt Johnson. Obtained certificate	
"	17th		Office Routine	
"	18th		Received DVSS approval for demobilize Sgt Lucas 14 VS. Ant Clothier obtained certificate for Capt B A Myhill RAVC	

(3)

Army Form C. 2118.

WAR DIARY

Capt A.D.V.S.

INTELLIGENCE SUMMARY. 3rd Cav Div

(Erase heading not required.)

Place	Date	Hour	Summary of Events and Information	Remarks and references to Appendices
NAMUR	MAY 19th		Inspected horses at arrival Cable Coy ENGIS for disposal to NAMUR to be evacuated to base. One horse kept to be re-inspected	
	20th		Inspected horse Camp	
	21st		Officers Ramline Arms at Cable Coy ENGIS closed above the last entraining dispatched to NAMUR	
			Two horses passed through the Camp 675 9	
			Despatched by Ease 664 9 Sick & destroyed 9 Returned to Unit 3 Lost 3. 12 horses Refd 20 & 13 MOS 23	
	22nd		Horses Refd. 23 & 19 got arms 9 13 M & 14th MRS & ENGIS	
	23rd		Horses Refd. Ole Moons or Starts to 39th MRS Lost [?]	
ENGIS	24th		Lt. [?] 13 M & 14 M MRS move to ENGIS above their Offices	
	25th		Dispatched sorry of horse Strupped Damages to bt Cav Div	
	26th		" "	
	27th		" "	
	28th		" "	
	29th		" "	
	30th		" "	

[signature]
Capt R.A.V.C.
A.D.V.S. 3rd Cav Div

www.ingramcontent.com/pod-product-compliance
Lightning Source LLC
Chambersburg PA
CBHW081555160426
43191CB00011B/1938